No Clients, No Job, No Problem

By Wayne Schoeneberg

Table of Contents

Forward

Wayne Schoeneberg's new book, **No Clients, No Job, No Problem,** is as much biography as it is a practical handbook. As a hornbook, it reveals the black letter law understanding of human nature. Mark Twain said, "Apparently no narrative that tells the facts of a man's life in the man's own words, can be uninteresting." And this little book is very interesting.

Timing is everything and the timing of the release of this treatise could not be better. Lawyers have been graduating from law schools in record numbers, and many are not easily finding a comfortable fit in an existing law firm or employment at all, for that matter. When I started Law School at the University of Missouri in 1962 I knew where I would practice law when (if?) I graduated and passed the Bar, and that's what happened. But after a year or two, that arrangement ended and I opened an office by myself.

Now all of the details of running a law practice and a business, which had previously been handled by the established law firm, became my responsibility. Over time it worked, but only with lots of trial and error and help and assistance from all the lawyers in the area. I think many of those lawyers had pity because they started the same way. I was never afraid to ask for help from another lawyer, and I was never refused a request by one. The lawyers were collegial then, even if you had just fought a tough case against each other. Wayne's book could have unraveled a tangle of problems that I worked through.

But things are different now with all of these new lawyers. I think many fresh from law school believe it shows weakness to ask other lawyers for help or advice. They are not particularly friendly with other lawyers and do not become friends. If a young (or not so young, but inexperienced) lawyer does not have the comforting cocoon and guidance of a mentor and/or law firm, what is he or she to do?

The answers lie in Wayne's book, a straightforward guidebook for the fledgling or the skeptical, wrought from his years of experience from setbacks, heartbreaks and anxieties but also from successes, conquests and triumphs.

Wayne Schoeneberg is a confident lawyer and coach. The wisdom collected in this book can relieve much of the anxiety that develops when we enter into an unfamiliar situation. Let's face it; law school doesn't give us the tools to deal with the nuts and bolts of a law practice. Time apparently doesn't permit the schools to teach the clear directions that Wayne provides for getting and retaining clients, developing and maintaining productive and loyal staff and growing an ethical, effective and financially successful practice. His insights will give guidance in making all of it succeed while keeping that important perspective and balance between home life and professional career. This book should be required reading and could be easily modified to become a law school textbook.

Robert M. Clayton II
Retired Circuit Judge
Hannibal, Missouri

Introduction

One day, I looked around me and couldn't believe what I saw. I was sitting in Paul Bocuse's restaurant near Lyon, France, having a wonderful lunch with the wife I had dreamed about all my life. I had been recognized as a leader in my profession many times over. I was already on any number of organizations "Top [fill in the blank] Lawyer" lists. I had a great practice and all of the money I needed.

However, when I started the practice of law, I had no job, no clients and no prospects, so I decided that there was only one option – success. Nothing makes a person want to succeed like survival, and that was where I was when I got out of law school.

As I was enjoying my successes over an eight-hundred-dollar lunch in France, I realized that there were thousands of lawyers struggling to get by. They were facing the same situation as I had done years ago with no job and no clients. For many years, lawyers had been coming to me with questions ranging from how to try a lawsuit, to how to deal with the day-to-day rigors of the practice of law. I had represented lawyers in matters ranging from disciplinary actions to divorces and criminal cases.

It occurred to me that by becoming a coach, I could reach out to and help even more lawyers overcome some of the huge roadblocks they would encounter. The more I coached, the more I saw the need to spread the good word. Being a lawyer can be financially and personally rewarding, but there are landmines along the way. There are things you need to do that might not be so evident. There are things to think about and situations to avoid. Even though my coaching career had spread out into other professions from entrepreneurs to actors, I will always have a special affinity for attorneys. I realized, though, that I couldn't coach everybody, so I decided to write this book.

This is a labor of love. It is a compilation of things I knew and things I have learned. Most of my lessons were learned the hard way. Some of the advice in this book is advice that I wish I had received years ago. Much of it comes from those lessons I learned when I was knocked to my knees, and that happened more than once. However, I got back up and pressed on. I didn't always learn from my first failure, but I also learned that failure isn't a failure until you quit trying.

This book is for you. Take what you want and leave the rest behind. I have no agenda here other than to try and help you succeed. I want all lawyers to succeed in this once proud profession, so that it may return to its deserved position of respect in the community.

Chapter 1

Purpose Driven Practice
What is Your Niche?

When people come out of law school, they frequently have a general idea of what they want to do. However, that generally changes pretty quickly. I know that I pictured myself as a tax attorney for a while. Circumstances changed that. My experience is that very few lawyers come out of school absolutely sure of what they want to do, get into one area of practice, and stay there the rest of their careers. Nevertheless, it is important to know what your niche is. It is important to know what you want to do and what your purpose is. If you don't know where you are going, how will you get there?

The practice of law is a difficult endeavor, and lawyers need to be involved in the part of the practice that they really enjoy. You are going to be putting in long hours, usually in less than glamorous surroundings. You are going to be isolated from your friends and family. So stop now and ask yourself some questions: What type of law would you love to practice if money was not an obstacle? What about the law do you love to do? What area of the law is so interesting to you that you find yourself reading about it, even though you don't have any cases or work in that field? That is your purpose as a lawyer. That is what you were meant to do as a lawyer. The sooner you come to grips with that, the happier you are going to be.

That does not mean you are going to start with that job. Economics may dictate that you take a job in some other field when you first graduate from law school. That's okay; don't give up the dream yet. There is still hope! It is also not unusual that when you first graduate, you don't have enough experience to know what you truly like to do. Within the first three years or so of practicing law, you will know for sure where your interests lie. It then becomes incumbent upon you to find a way to work in that area. If you do not, you will never find fulfillment as a lawyer. Let me say that a different way: square pegs don't fit into round holes. I have spent a great deal of time coaching lawyers who make a lot of money, but are unhappy because they are not in a field they like. I can think of nothing worse than spending my life doing something that does not appeal to me.

So as soon as you can, figure it out. Then when you do, act on it. You may even have to take a cut in pay, but it will save you a thousand headaches and grouchy exchanges with your friends and family.

I've helped many attorneys, young and old, discover their true purpose and find the satisfaction that they never knew was possible. When you find your niche or your purpose, you are going to find that you are really good at it. The reason you are really good at it is because you have a passion for it. Since you have a passion for it, you will do it better, accomplish more, and be happier. I predict that you will even make more money! I'll try talking about attitude a little later, but let me say this right away: a happy lawyer has a better earning capacity than an unhappy lawyer, all other things being equal. When you are passionate about something you are doing, you simply perform better.

Passion is a necessary element of success. A life without passion is empty. You have to be passionate about your personal life and your professional life. Passion heightens enjoyment. Passion motivates. Passion causes you to put more energy into something than what is required. It is more than just enthusiasm or excitement. Passion is ambition. It materializes into actions to put as much heart, mind, wanting, and soul, into something as possible.

Passion is not the same as purpose. Purpose is about being rather than doing. Passion is the "why" behind your motivation. If you find your purpose, you will find your passion. Your life purpose is about staying connected. Your law purpose is about being successful. Don't let yourself get pigeonholed into something you don't like. This is a career that you have chosen as your life's work. It has to fulfill you. It has to satisfy you. It has made you smile. It should bless you with rewards. You should wake up each morning anxious to go to work. People are paying you to do this. How great is that! You should be excited every day. If you are not, you have not found your purpose; you haven't found your niche.

Many times people are encouraged not to be dreamers. I encourage people to dream all the time. Dream about your future life, paint a picture of it, and move yourself into it. Envision the lawyer you want to be, and then be that lawyer. It is almost necessary for you to do that in order to have success. You have to create a visual image of who you want to be, and then become that person by working towards that image every day.

Who do you want to be? Write it down. Do it now. I'm serious. Take a minute, or put this book down and don't come back to it until you can answer that question. Who do you want to be?

Write down your answer in detail. Paint a picture with words. Describe your clothes, your office, your house, car, boat, maybe even your plane. Where will you live? Will you be married? Will you have children? What will your law practice be like? Will you be a sole practitioner, a partner in a small firm, or maybe a partner in a huge firm? You control your destiny. You are what you think. Now think. Now write it down.

Once you have painted the picture, you can move forward into that. As you go along, you can adjust your dreams to your reality, or your reality to your dreams. Dreaming is the first step. Picture who you want to be five years from now, ten years from now, and then be that person. Create a picture. It can be words on a page or a visual image in your head. Either way, you are a product of what you think. The fact that you are sitting where you are sitting and reading this book is a result of every thought you have had all your life prior to this immediate moment.

So when you are thinking about your future, remember to think about the great things in store for you.

One important step in finding your niche is understanding that you can't be all things to all people. As much as there is an inclination when you come out of law school to tell everybody that you do everything, you just can't. First of all, the practice of law is so varied now, and there are so many different fields of law, that it is impossible to cover all of the bases. I saw a website of a local lawyer who listed at least fifty different things he did. They included wills, trusts, estates, product liability, premises liability, trademark, copyright, automobile accidents, truck accidents, divorce, medical malpractice, contracts, civil litigation, (see where I'm going with this?) criminal, and on and on. He then broke the criminal field down into every possible case type from traffic to homicide. Nobody in their right mind is going to choose a lawyer who claims to do all of that. No one person can do all of that and do it well.

In the state of Missouri where I work, lawyers cannot hold themselves out as specialists in any particular field. That does not mean they cannot specialize in certain areas. They just can't say they are a "specialist." It is one of those silly rules that governing bodies try to impose on people when they don't know how to handle a problem. In addition, lawyer advertising is a problem. But it isn't a problem I am here to talk about. If you live in one of the states that do not allow you to "specialize", then don't violate the rule by advertising it. Just tell people what kind of cases you handle. I handle criminal and personal injury cases. Am I a "specialist"? No, of course not. But I seldom handle other types of cases, and people know that. In fact, I just told you that, and I did it without calling myself a "specialist." Where there is a will, there is a way. My point here is that you need to let people know what you do.

If you are a criminal lawyer, tell people that when they ask you. If you want to work with divorce cases, say so. People want to know. Even if they don't, you want them to know. I hate to leave a meeting or gathering thinking that there might be someone there who is looking for a criminal lawyer and all they know about me is that I "practice law."

If it really is your passion, you will be talking about it anyway. I had the occasion to meet Ralph Nader at one of his birthday parties. I can't remember which one and it does not matter. But I assure you that Ralph Nader was a passionate guy. You did not leave his company without learning about what was on his mind. That is what you need to tell people about. That will be what keeps you going. When they know what you do, people will come to you and refer clients to you.

Imagine when you meet somebody at a meeting, they ask what kind of law you do, and you say, "I have a general practice, I handle just about everything." They don't know what that means. What is a general practice, anyway? Do you do wills? No? How about bank mergers? No? Well, tell them what you do. Don't be afraid that they aren't looking for that type of lawyer. They probably aren't looking for any lawyer right then. But leave them with an identity for your practice. Let them know that you are a lawyer who does [Fill in the blank]. I assure you that non-lawyers do not know what you mean by a "general practice."

So your niche is key. Your niche is different from your purpose. You have to find your purpose first, but your niche is what you actually do. If you want to be a trial lawyer, then be a trial lawyer. Make that your dream. Maybe you want to be a transactional lawyer or a real estate lawyer? Perhaps you want to work in intellectual property or even do medical malpractice work? No matter what it is, you need to find your niche.

Years ago, I was on the Board of Governors of the Missouri Association of Trial Attorneys. Some new lawyers moved into the Kansas City area, and they held themselves out as doing nothing other than medical malpractice. That was it. They didn't do criminal, divorce, auto accidents, or anything other than medical malpractice.

I still remember when they came on the scene. People actually smirked about it. "Who are these people coming in and saying they do nothing but medical malpractice? They come here, and they're starting at ground zero. Don't they understand how complicated that is?" Today, that firm is one of the biggest plaintiff's personal injury firms in the country. They succeeded because they found what they liked to do. They had a passion in what they wanted to do. They were specific about what they did, and people started relying on them. People started referring business to them because they were good at what they did. They were good at what they did because they followed the rules you have read about here. They had a purpose. They picked a niche. They dreamed about who they wanted to be, and they became that.

I'm a trial lawyer. At this point in my practice, I primarily handle criminal work. For years, I did personal injury and criminal law. Anybody who knew me knew what I did. That is who I was: a personal injury and criminal lawyer. When people wanted to make a referral on a personal injury case, they called me. If people wanted to make a referral on a criminal case, they called me. I was the guy to go to for those cases in my geographical area, and they knew that.

I served on the Board of Governors of the Missouri Association of Trial Attorneys. MATA, as it is known, is the personal injury trial lawyers group for Missouri. It is the State arm of the American Association for Justice (AAJ). That is what used to be called The Association of Trial Lawyers of America (ATLA). Then politicians picked up on the term "trial lawyers" and vilified them in every election. So ATLA stuck its proverbial middle finger in the air and changed its name to the The American Association of Justice.

Whatever its name is, it is an organization of attorneys who spend their time representing injured people. They are dedicated to enforcing the rights of people who are victims of the negligence and wrongdoing of others. Not only do they work for them in the courtroom, they also spend a lot of time, money, and resources, working with the legislatures on the state level and Congress on the national level to try and stop draconian legislation that limits the rights of injured people to seek redress through the courts.

I still do some work in personal injury. When people come to me for that, I'll handle their case. But I am not out looking for those cases anymore. Between coaching, speaking, and criminal cases, I have all I can handle. (Oh, yes, I guess writing books should be in there, too.) The point I want to make is that I am doing what I am passionate about. At sixty-seven years old, I have more joy, enthusiasm and energy than people far younger than I am.

There are lawyers who do family law, so when a case comes in to me for family law; I refer them to lawyers that specialize in that field. If a case comes in to me for a bankruptcy, I know who to refer that to. I'm out there as an extension of these people's law firms, helping them get cases because I know what they are known for and that they're good. I am a field representative for those lawyers. Why? Because I want to refer people I know to the right kind of lawyer. If I know what work you do, and you are good at it, I'll send you a case. But if someone asks me about a lawyer, and I don't know what type of cases he or she handles, I have to say nothing. So you see, you need to have that niche. People need to know what you do and that you are good at it (we'll talk more about being good at it later). Then they will send you business.

People who are really good at what they do have a passion for it, or at least they did at one point. Often times in the law profession that passion fades, and people become almost routine in what they do. They've seen a particular case a hundred times before, they know exactly what it is about, they can pretty well predict the outcome, and they go through the motions. They've lost their passion and their enjoyment of their work. I coach lawyers who feel like that on a regular basis. When I go into a courtroom and address another lawyer, I can almost guarantee you that when I say, "How's it going?" he will give me a forlorn look followed by some general, if not specific, complaint.

Remember, I am talking to a man or woman who voluntarily enrolled in law school, paid tuition and fees, lived in a constant state of persecution for three years, got a degree, and then voluntarily started practicing law. Nobody forced him or her to do this. They were once so excited about it that they couldn't wait for the morning to come. Now, they hate it. Nobody should live like that. They are doing their clients a disservice because the clients are not getting the full attention they deserve. They are also doing themselves a disservice because this is the only life they are ever going to get to live, and they are wasting it doing something that does not bring them joy.

So here is another moment I want you to stop and think. Is this really what you want to do with your life? Are you ready to dive in up to your neck and give it your all every working minute of every working day? That is really what you are pledging to do when you take that oath. You are swearing that your clients are never going to get anything but your best. Notice though, that I said "every working moment of every working day." I do not believe that your practice should consume you. I will discuss that in more detail later.

Here's what I think about: On a daily basis, I have this great profession that allows me to practice law. I went to law school to become a lawyer. It was important to me back then to become a lawyer, and it is important to me now to be a lawyer. It allows me to practice law and get paid for it. I have a passion for my cases because I really enjoy it.

A part of that is that I am selective about the cases that I take, and I would encourage anybody to do the same. If you don't like a case, don't take it. If you don't like a client, don't take it. You have to maintain the passion. You have to look at each case individually, and you have to say, "How can I make this case different in order to help my client?" If you have that passion, you are not just going through the motions.

I see this all the time in the criminal practice; people take a case in, talk to the client, call the prosecuting attorney to find out what kind of deal they can get, and then they take the client in and plead him or her guilty. First of all, that is not satisfying. You are not really accomplishing anything, and part of the whole concept of "purpose" is that you have to be fulfilled in life. No matter how much money you make, if you are not fulfilled, you are not happy, and if you are not happy, it is not worth doing.

A practice without passion is doomed to fail. If you don't have passion, you are not going to get up in the morning and go to work with the right attitude. You are not going to give off the right vibes to potential clients. You are not going to pay attention to the details that you need to pay attention to. You have to have the passion to practice. You have to come to work every day excited. If you get your right niche and you know your purpose, then you are living your dream.

In order to keep the right mindset, the first thing I do is live in the present. The past is the past, and as a trial lawyer, you have to quickly determine that you are not going to dwell on the past, especially if you do criminal trial work. It is a difficult kind of work, and in a lot of trials clients end up being convicted. That is just a fact of life. If you are not getting any guilty verdicts, you are not trying enough cases. Certainly, you want to get not guilty verdicts. If you do trial work you are always "in it to win it."

However, if you start counting "wins" and "losses", you are soon going to be more concerned with your won/loss record than your client's interests. Remember that you are their voice in the legal system. They came to you to say the things they want said about their position, just in a more eloquent and relevant way. When you start keeping track of how many cases you win versus how many cases you lost, it becomes about you and not the client. And that, my dear reader, is wrong.

Let's get back to attitude. I get up every morning, and I am very thankful for that day. I start my day before I get out of bed with being thankful for that day. I look around and realize that this is the only time that I'm going to have the opportunity to live that day, and I decide to make the best of it. That is the frame of mind I start out in.

If during the day I get to a point where chaos has broken out around me, and I feel like things are running amok, I do what I call "centering myself." I find some time alone. Sometimes I will go into a witness room outside a courtroom. I just walk in, and I close the door. I'm the only person in the room. I clear my mind of everything, and I think about absolutely nothing. I don't think about the telephone calls that need to be returned. I don't think about the prosecutors who are being unreasonable. I don't think about the trial that is coming up next week. I don't think about the accounts receivable. I think about absolutely nothing. It takes about ten minutes, but it is as good as a power nap. After that ten-minute period of time when I clear my mind, I'm able to come out ready to start the day again. It is like a fresh start to the day. No matter what has happened up until that moment in time, it has happened and there is no changing it.

I realize every day that the things that happen are just events in my life. They are not good events, nor are they bad events. Each thing that happens is a part of a series of events that weaves the fabric of my life. That perspective helps me get through days that are particularly challenging. There are days that are more challenging than others, but remember that each event, each person that you meet, and each place that you go, gives you an opportunity to better your place in life. All of life is about opportunity. This day, the one you are in right now as you read this book, is the only opportunity you are going to have to live this day. If you aren't enjoying yourself right now, if you don't think that reading this book right now is the best use of your time, put it down and come back to it when the time is right. This is your moment. You will never have this moment again. Wring everything out of it that you can. If that means putting down this book for a while, do it, and go do what makes you happy and fulfilled.

Okay, you are either still with me, or you just came back. Let's get on with living a great, fun and fulfilled life. Here are some more simple suggestions. I mention these suggestions about happiness because having a job and clients is not going to fulfill you if you are not happy. If you aren't happy, clients and a job won't make you happy. Happiness comes from within. If you are happy first, you stand a better chance of getting a job and clients. I know that sound too simple. That is the problem. Most people make it too complicated.

I have two sort of imaginary jars on my dresser. One has a plus sign on it and one has a minus sign on it. Before I go to bed at night, I imagine myself tearing a page off the calendar. Picture one of those calendars you see in old movies that just has a big number in the middle. I tear that page off the imaginary calendar, crumple it up into a ball, and then I have to make a decision. Which jar do I put it in? Do I put it in the jar with the plus sign meaning that I spent the day well, or do I put it in the jar with the minus sign indicating that I wasted that day and did not use it all up. I go through every day making sure that I can drop that paper into the jar with the plus sign. Knowing that imaginary jar is there motivates me every day.

My primary purpose and value in life is fun. I believe that when the Man gave me the tickets for the ride on planet Earth, He said, "You are only going to do this once. Have the best time you can." That has always been my goal, and that works for me.

Chapter 2

The Ethical Practice
It Is Never Worth Taking Shortcuts

The first thing that every lawyer in every jurisdiction needs to know is what the rules of that jurisdiction are pertaining to conduct. There are rules promulgated by the American Bar Association that are almost universally adopted by the states. But you should be aware that each state can have, and usually does have, some rules peculiar to their state. There are rules that cover relationships with clients. There are rules that cover relationships with other lawyers. There are rules that cover relationships with the courts. There are rules that deal with advertising. There are rules that deal with what boards you can serve on, or how you can serve on a board. There are rules that deal with your accounts that handle client's money.

All of those rules are out there, and the first and fundamental thing if you are going to practice in a jurisdiction, is that you need to know what that state's or that jurisdiction's rules are. There are also rules that govern practice in federal court, rules of ethics for lawyers in federal courts that may or may not be different in slight respects from jurisdiction to jurisdiction. I recently attended a webinar, and the lecturer was pointing out how the rules pertaining to client contact during a deposition varied from one federal court to another. A lawyer was sanctioned in one jurisdiction for doing the very same thing he did in his own jurisdiction. The very first thing that every lawyer owes himself or herself is to know what those rules are.

There are two types of offenses. One is an intentional offense. The other is an act or omission that is negligent or a result of some other mistake. Let's talk a little bit about both.

An intentional, ethical offense is, of course, inexcusable. Stealing from clients is one such offense. The punishment can range from disbarment to reprimand, but I am pretty sure most lawyers who steal from clients get disbarred. It only seems right. So how about the lawyer who mishandles a client's funds? Well, there are some variations on this.

I have seen lawyers who take too long to pay out a client's settlement because they are "borrowing" from the client. Not allowed! I have seen cases where lawyers are sloppy bookkeepers and bounce checks to clients for settlement distributions. Not allowed! Go now. Yes, put down this book, and do an Internet search for Rule 1.15 of the American Bar Association Rules of Professional Conduct. Read it and come back. I'll wait.

Okay, did you read it thoroughly? You are dealing with "other people's money." It is not yours, and if you treat it like yours, the people who allow you to have a license to practice law in your jurisdiction are going to come down hard, very hard on you. Don't do it, not for a penny, ever. Okay? Got it?

It is almost as bad to unintentionally or unknowingly violate some ethical rule, as it is to do it intentionally. I mean, you are a lawyer, and you are supposed to know the law. The rules are part of the law. It just seems a little lame to claim that you "didn't know" that what you were doing was a violation of the rules of your profession, which is a profession wherein we help people live life within the rules.

If you know the rules, they're going to be there in your mind every day as you do your things. They are going to govern your behavior. That is so important, especially now. Missouri has changed the way they deal with ethical violations in the course of my practice. Now there is an obligation on the part of a lawyer who sees what he believes to be an ethical violation being committed by another lawyer, to report that lawyer to the Disciplinary Committee. That means that if I see or suspect that you are doing something unethical, or you do something to me that I believe is an ethical violation in a case, I have to report that, or else I violate the rules! That little rule can trip anybody up. If you are doing your best in a case, and you violate some ethical rule by mistake, your opponent has an obligation to report you. Think about that. If he does not, he has violated an ethical rule. It would be so foolish for you to unintentionally violate one of the rules of professional conduct. So my first rule on ethics is to know the rules.

Years ago, there was a high-profile prosecution of a large drug ring in the Southern District of Illinois, United States Federal Court. There were a large number of defendants, and I happened to have some ties to some of these defendants. Early on, while the other defendants were being rounded up, three guys showed up in my office one day to talk about the case. They wanted me to represent one of the defendants who had not yet been apprehended.

They had a bag with them, an overseas bag is what we would call it in the Army, like a big duffle bag, except it zipped on the top. They came in and plopped that down, took their seats around the conference table, and then we talked for a while. We talked a little bit about representing the client, what some of the facts were, what it would take to defend the case, and what the case was about.

Then one of them opened up this bag, and he said, "There's a million dollars in that bag." I had no way of telling whether there was a million dollars in there or not, but I saw enough hundred-dollar bills to impress me. The bag was clearly big enough to hold a million dollars in hundred dollar bills. I thought, "Yeah, I'd love to charge that much, but I'm not sure I can convince myself I'm worth that much." I said, "What's the million dollars for?" He said, "That's to pass around to the judges and the prosecutors in this case. We'll pay whatever your fee is, but this is for you to use." I looked at him, and he continued, "That's the way we do business. There's a million dollars in other lawyer's hands too, so there's enough money to go around. We just want you to buy this case off," he said.

This offer didn't tempt me for a second, but that is the kind of thing that you can be faced with. There are enough ethical questions here to make for an entire bar exam. I just explained to him that, first of all, I wasn't interested in that. And secondly, I didn't know what jurisdictions they practiced in, but down here in Missouri, or in the Southern

District of Illinois, it just isn't done that way. With that we parted company. To their credit, they were professional about it. We all shook hands, I wished them the best, and they left. By the way, the least amount of time any of the defendants in that case got was twenty years. The case took place before the Federal sentencing guidelines went into effect.

Those are the types of things you have to watch out for. There could certainly be a big temptation in that situation. An old friend of mine fell prey to a scheme wherein he was asked by a client to take a suitcase from the United States to Switzerland. The suitcase had hundreds of thousands of dollars in it. He took the bait and was promptly arrested when he got to Switzerland. That was about fifteen years ago. He did time in Federal prison and still does not have his license to practice law back. My advice to people is to act each day and conduct each day as if someone is looking over your shoulder. There is nothing imprisoning about doing that if you are not going to do something wrong.

I had a situation one time, which I found to be an interesting event. When I did a lot of personal injury work, a guy who said that he had been rear-ended in an automobile collision came into my office one day. He said a friend referred him, but he couldn't remember the friend's name. That is very common, so I didn't pay too much attention to that.

During that period of time, a lot of us used chiropractors that we would refer people to if they came in with a back or a neck injury. We obviously had our favorite chiropractors that we would send them to. This guy came in and claimed that he had been rear-ended and that he had a heart problem. A heart problem just does not come from the type of accident that he described. I explained to him that I didn't believe his story supported a heart problem, but he was still sure that he had one. He kept asking me if I had a chiropractor I could send him to. I said, "No, I really don't have a chiropractor I can send you to for a heart problem. You should go to a heart doctor, and I don't know any heart doctors. Pick one and go to them."

He was in my office for probably an hour insisting that I send him to a chiropractor, and I was insisting that I wasn't going to do it. I ended the interview by telling him that I wasn't going to sign his case up at that time, but if he went to a heart doctor and found a heart problem as a result of his accident, he should come back. Then I would be glad to get his medical records and see if we could make a case based on those.

He took off, leaving his papers, interestingly enough. It is very unusual for the clients to bring an accident report when they come in, but he did. I took this and the other papers he had left behind, and I sent them to the address shown on the accident report. However, they came back to me saying that there was no such address. About a week later, half a dozen lawyers and half a dozen chiropractors were indicted. Perhaps the guy who had visited me was sent in there to see if I would take the bait. I don't know if that was the case, but I didn't have to worry about it. I never heard from the guy again.

Your reputation is either going to help you or haunt you. It is critically important. It is actually more important among the lawyers and judges than it is among clients. Lay people have a different view of lawyers' reputations. I believe lay people think that all lawyers are of questionable ethics, which is unfortunate. We get that reputation because of the way we act. Your reputation of honesty and ethics will help you or kill you with other lawyers and judges. There are some lawyers who are known for their lack of ethics, and nobody wants to deal with them. Nobody gives them any slack in anything. Nobody trusts them, and it just makes their life a little more difficult.

Perhaps most lawyers have no reputation one way or the other for ethical behavior. Lawyers who have a good reputation for ethical behavior are going to get breaks, interestingly enough, from other lawyers. If somebody I trust calls me up and says, "Look Wayne, I can't make it to a scheduled deposition because…" he does not even have to give me the "because." If he tells me he can't make it, I know that he's got a legitimate reason and that he's telling me the truth. There is no sense hassling with him. We'll just reschedule it.

If you have a bad ethical reputation, however, and you call me up and say, "I can't make it to the deposition," or "my client can't make it," the first thing I do is suspect what you are telling me. I suspect that you are trying to get something over on me, and I'm going to be less willing to cooperate with you in giving you what you want.

The same goes for judges. If I call a judge and tell him or her that I can't try a case on a certain day because I'm in a conflict of some sort, the judge is not going question that. Judges know that I have a reputation of being ready for trial. In addition, I have a reputation of being honest with the courts. I'm not going to make up some story as to why I can't get to trial on a case, be in court on a certain day, or be somewhere else. It is not worth it to my reputation.

Your reputation also slops over on your clients. Maybe the client of the lawyer who has a bad reputation really can't make it that day, but I don't trust the lawyer because he has a reputation for being sleazy. The consequence is that I'm not going to give that lawyer a break. I understand that I'm making it more difficult on his client, but I have my client to represent first.

You see how your reputation is going to be important? Your reputation with the clients is important because they talk in the community. Never suggest or even imply to a client that you are going to do something that is unethical. That reputation is going to spread. You may think it is just between you and the client, but it is not. They're going to go out in the community and tell others, and it is going to come back to haunt you.

I once had a client come in on a case telling me that he was going to hire me because he knew I was close with a certain judge. He said that another lawyer had told him this judge would throw the case out for a two thousand dollar bribe. This client thought that since I was close to the judge, it would be better if I handled the case. I did know the judge, and I thought it was a shame that someone was saying that about him. He certainly gave every break he could to people charged with a crime, but that was not unethical. I never saw him do or say anything that made me believe he had taken or would take a bribe. I told this man that there was nothing I knew about the judge that led me to believe he was crooked, but the client was willing to pay a hefty fee for handling the case. It looked like a weak case to me, but I was not taking it just the same. I wasn't even about to suggest to this potential client that I would bribe a judge. My reputation was worth more to me than whatever that client was going to pay.

Clients frequently misunderstand your role as a lawyer. Your role as a lawyer is to take the facts as they are and advocate them as best as you can in the best interest of your client. I have had clients, however, who come in and tell me that they have done something or committed some act or offense, and then they ask me how they can present it so that it does not look like they have done it.

In a criminal case, the state has the burden of proof. We don't have to put on any evidence. For example, I recently had a case where the residence of the defendant was in question. If he lived at the place where they arrested him, it was more probable than not that he would be found guilty of possessing the drugs that were found there. If he lived somewhere else, it was at least arguable that those were not his drugs.

When I interviewed him, he told me that he really did live somewhere else. I asked him where he lived, and he gave me the name of a lady who he said could verify his residence. I went and spoke with her, and she told me that he indeed did live there with her. I took her deposition because I wanted to make sure the prosecutor knew that I had a good witness who could say that he lived somewhere else.

The day of trial was the next time I spoke with the lady again. When she showed up at trial, she pulled me aside and said, "I have to tell you that I was lying about what I said. He never did live with me. I am afraid to get on the stand and lie." "Great!" I thought. "Now you tell me?"

That meant I had to get in a big discussion with the client about using this witness. I could not knowingly put a person on the stand who was going to tell a lie. I can't go into what the client said here because that might be disclosing privileged information, but the decision was made not to use the lady.

From time to time, clients are going to ask you to bend the rules. There are as many possible situations as you can imagine. It might be on something as insignificant as witnessing a signature you didn't actually see, but you still can't do it. You have to explain to your clients that first and foremost, you are honest and ethical. You cannot allow them to make you bend your ethics.

Another thing you have to avoid is giving your client the impression that you can "fix" things. We all know that when we talk about fixing a ticket, there is nothing crooked about it. It is a plea bargain. They reduce it to something else, and the person pays the fine. That's "fixing" a ticket. We all know that there is nothing unethical or even special about that process. It is done very openly.

However, when clients talk about "fixing" something, they're frequently talking about going outside the judicial system, like paying a person off, or calling in a favor, in other words doing something that bends the rules. That is what I am talking about. Remember, if what you are about to do is something you don't want everybody to know about, don't do it. You can call in a favor that is owed to you by someone, but it can't be in order to do something shady.

If I call a prosecuting attorney who I have known for a long time and ask him to pay special attention to a case as a favor to me, that's okay. If I ask him or her because we are friends, to not file a charge against a certain client, that's okay. It is his or her discretion. But if I ask that same prosecutor to not call a certain witness, or to disclose some fact to me that I should not have, that is wrong.

There will frequently be pressure from clients to do something that isn't quite on the up-and-up with the rules, and you must avoid the temptation to give in. This pressure can come from a client in a criminal case or some businessman you represent in a transaction. It may be something as simple as a request to "look the other way." I know that lawyers who defend large corporations have to deal with these situations a lot. In some office, there is some person that the lawyer has never met. That person is trying to hide a document or change a report. The lawyer discovers it. Does he go along with it? He shouldn't.

Sometimes it would be the very easy way to go, and sometimes the result would make you look good to your client and his or her friends. You might even look good in the community, as long as no one knows what you did to achieve that result. It is those times that you have to ask yourself whether you want peace inside, or you want to spend your time worrying, not only about getting caught, but also having to deal with yourself on a daily basis.

The lure of money can be very appealing. I go back to the question of the big drug case and the million dollars in cash. I have no idea what they were going to pay me in attorney's fees. I'm sure it would have been more than a hundred thousand dollars, but it just isn't worth it. There is a constant temptation as a lawyer to let money mislead you.

Another area where lawyers get into trouble way too often is dealing with client's funds. Lawyers frequently hold client's money in an escrow account. It happens a lot in personal injury cases. If I settle a personal injury case for a million dollars, the insurance company sends me a draft for a million dollars, my client and I sign it, and we put it in my escrow account. The client doesn't have any access to that escrow account, but I have access to it, and it is my obligation after that draft clears to pay my client what he is owed in a timely manner. I deduct my attorney's fees, and any legitimate costs advanced, I pay any medical bills that have legitimate liens filed, and then that client gets a net payout. My fee may be 300,000 dollars, the other expenses come out, and in the end the client is entitled to 600,000 dollars.

Time and time again, I see disciplinary actions wherein lawyers dip into those funds. It is no different than embezzlement. They take the client's funds to pay their own expenses, I guess with the thought that they can cover it at some point, that the client won't know, or they'll put the client off saying that, "the draft hasn't cleared yet." The lure of money ruins an awful lot of lawyers. There are going to be times in your career as a lawyer when your own funds are short (hopefully that will not happen to you if you read this book and engage me as your coach). You must not let one of those moments ruin your career.

Chapter 3
Building a Debt Free Business

Are You Willing to Take Financial Responsibility?

Your financial responsibility as a lawyer is extremely important. As a business professional licensed by your state, you are held to a higher standard than others. People look at you, or should be able to look at you and other lawyers, with respect. You have a duty to yourself, your family, and your clients, to be financially independent. When you have financial stability, it keeps you from making poor decisions where money is involved.

To achieve financial stability, rule number one is to live within your means. Rule number two is to invest for your retirement. Rule number three is to avoid excessive spending. That is sort of rule number one re-stated. You also have to have a plan for how you are going to build your business. Without a plan, you will go nowhere. Planning is key. Remember that you have an ethical and moral duty to be financially independent, and without really being able to quote chapters and verse, I know that admonition shows up in the scriptures of many religions.

You have a duty to your client to be financially independent. Does that sound a little odd? It is true though. If you are not financially independent, there is that temptation that we discussed in the last chapter. If you are not financially independent, you are weak. If you are weak, you are at the mercy of temptations to do things you would not normally do.

There is a temptation when you are dealing with other people's money. Nothing will get you in more trouble than other people's money. When you are not financially independent, you are tempted to take a short cut if it will make you a quick dollar. If you find yourself under financial pressure, you start thinking more about your interests than you do your client's interests.

Here is a simple example. One lawyer can only handle a certain amount of cases. That number will vary depending on a lot of things. Some of the factors are the lawyer's individual skills, his or her capacity to produce, and the complexity of the matter. I submit that one lawyer can handle more traffic tickets than products liability cases.

Once that lawyer passes the optimal number of cases, his or her performance suffers.

There are too many things that need to be done, too many phone calls, too many pleadings, too many papers to draft, etc. I am sure that all seems pretty clear to you. But when you find yourself financially strapped, there is a temptation to take the quick fix of taking in more cases at almost any price just to ease the cash flow. Don't do it!

Let me make myself clear; by "financially independent" I do not mean being rich or wealthy. I mean you must have your finances under control by using some of the concepts I talk about in this book. Live within your means, invest wisely, and have a plan.

Another thing you have to do is to establish a relationship with a financial advisor early on. Six months out of law school is not too early. You might not have made a penny if you started in your own practice, but establish a relationship with a good, trusted financial advisor. Start early and put money away, because in private practice you are going to have ebbs and flows, feast and famine. It happens to everybody in the private practice, and you have to plan for it. Set money aside. Do not just set aside that which you can afford. Set aside more than you can afford. Pay yourself first. Make your financial comfort a priority. I promise you that having a cash reserve will give you a better feeling in the long run than having a big boat or fancy car.

My goal is to always live within my means. I have spent a lot of money in my life on boats, cars, travels, and motorcycles, just to name a few things I enjoy. There is no question about it. I don't, however, spend money I don't have. When I was younger and times were tougher, I drove an old car. I still drive an old car, as a matter of fact, but I drove an even older car then. Now I can drive any car I want. I just choose to drive the one I have. It gets me from place to place.

Over the course of your career, you will see one lawyer and then the next rise to a level of prominence. Beware if that is you. Keep in mind it won't last forever. There is a lawyer in our community who is the current high-profile lawyer. This poor fellow just got a "Not Guilty" verdict on a high profile case. On his way home that night, he was in a minor accident. Because he is the current high-profile lawyer, the press was called. Yep! He was charged with driving under the influence of alcohol, and there on the nightly television news was a picture of him at the accident scene and the crushed front end of his Bentley. You can imagine the fun everybody had with that.

Just remember you owe it to yourself, your family, and your clients, to be financially independent.

For example: If you are in the personal injury business, and somebody offers you a hundred thousand dollars, that is going to be a 33,000-dollar fee. Perhaps you know in your heart that the case is worth 200,000 dollars, but you could probably talk your client into taking a hundred thousand dollars, and if you need the quick money, you are probably not going to push for the 200,000 dollars. You are going to look around and say, "Well, you know, a hundred thousand dollars is a good settlement, and we'd have to wait six more months to get 200,000 dollars." Your financial situation affects you, and that affects your clients. That is why financial independence is so important.

Not paying what you owe in taxes is a big stumbling block for lawyers. It is a pickle that lawyers get themselves into from time to time, and it is just not worth it. The state of Missouri has given me a license to do what I like and get paid for it. They don't ask a lot from me. They ask me to follow the rules of ethics, and aside from that and paying my dues, they don't ask anything else of me other than to pay the tax on the money that I earn.

Here's where a problem comes in. When you are a young lawyer and you are in practice for yourself, in other words, you are not an employee with somebody withholding taxes, social security, and the like, from your paycheck and giving you a net paycheck, you have to pay estimated taxes each quarter. If you haven't put anything aside when it comes to the end of that quarter, you look around and think, "Well, gee, I really don't have the money to pay those taxes. I'll just defer it to the next quarter." Of course what happens is that the next quarter you don't have the money either because you haven't planned for it, or you haven't set it aside. That is all the more reason to have a financial planner and have a financial plan.

Another scenario that comes around is that the first and second year of your practice, you make an okay living and are paying your taxes. Then, your third year, you make a ton of money, three times the amount that you made before, but you don't pay your estimated taxes because suddenly you are living large. Whereas you and your spouse were scrimping along in a little apartment and barely making ends meet, you are suddenly making a lot of money. You go out and buy a house, you each buy a new car, and you spend all of that money that you should have been paying on your estimated taxes. Then comes tax time, and you don't have the money.

There are two ways you can go at this point. One way is you get a tax lien filed against you. You file your tax returns, you don't pay the money, and you get the tax lien. Of course that gets published. Other people see it and immediately know that you are in trouble. That has an effect. It goes back to your reputation for honesty, integrity, and your financial responsibility. The other way that some lawyers choose to go about it is to not file a tax return at all!

Let me tell you a story. There is a man that I have known since law school. He was a contemporary of mine. He is one of the best trial lawyers that I know. He served in Vietnam, got decorated with the Silver Star for Valor, and had a great practice, but he spent more money than he should have. He failed to file tax returns for a couple of years and ended up getting indicted by the Federal government. He lost his law license and ended up in jail. What a tragedy. He finally got his law license back after a number of years of not practicing, but he ruined a great progression of a wonderful career.

Paying taxes is distasteful. I know it is. However, it is a necessary thing. I don't understand why a lawyer would not file his tax returns, but indeed, it happens. You have to pay your taxes. You have to stay up with your estimated taxes if you are self-employed. Also, remember to pay your payroll taxes if you have employees. That is not your money anyway. You are withholding that from your employees. (Remember the warnings about other people's money.) Do not fail to pay your taxes. It is the sure road to disaster.

It is extremely important that attorneys take care of their money. Lawyers, unfortunately, have a feeling that we're smart in all areas, but that isn't always the case. Investing money is a special field, and unless you are particularly educated in investments, you should turn that over to an expert. Again, you want to turn it over to somebody you trust, somebody you have vetted. In your first six months of practice, even though you are barely bringing anything home, you should sit down with a financial planner. By then you should have networked sufficiently that you should have met any number of financial advisors. Find a professional advisor with a good track record, ask your friends, ask older lawyers who are more successful, and find a good financial advisor. If you are only putting away a few bucks a month, start saving. Do not be concerned that you only have a small amount to put away. That will not put off a good financial planner. A good one will see that as an opportunity to help you build a fortune and become a good and valued client.

One reason why you turn it over to an expert is that you don't want to spend a lot of your time, which is basically how you earn your money, managing your finances. But you can't just turn your money over to someone without monitoring their performance and holding them accountable. You have to pay attention. You have to get involved. Investing at an early age is an absolute necessity. Lawyers fail to do it on a regular basis, and by the time they hit fifty, they start to panic and they start acting in a financially irresponsible way. That is why early investing is important. Get professional advice and set money aside on a regular, I would say monthly, basis. It is never too early to start planning for retirement.

As a part of your financial planning, you have to have two budgets. First of all, sit down and figure out what the minimum cost is to operate your household. Write down everything that you spend over a course of two or three months. Those are your basic necessary expenses. They have to be paid. This includes your rent, utilities, and food. It also includes what are you going to pay for your transportation, insurance, and how much you are going to invest. Set up that budget and live by it.

Then you have to go to your office and do the same thing there. Your office also has necessities that it is going to demand of you every month, and you have to have that money there. I will admit that it is hard to do. You have to sit down and figure out the fixed expenses that are absolute necessities. You have to put some money in savings, which has to go there as non-discretionary spending. That is a must because there are going to be times when you look around, and you can't believe that no clients are coming in the door. If you have money set aside, you are not going to panic. Then you are going to be able to make it through those times, and your business and professional decisions during those periods of time are going to be sounder than if you are in a financial crunch.

There is a problem with planning. It has to reflect reality. A banker once told me, "I have never seen a business plan submitted to me, or that I have reviewed, that takes into account the tough years in the short-term future. Every business plan that I see has a constant upward trend line of income and profits."

That is just not reality. Reality is that you are going to have some glitches in your trend line, and you have to budget for that. Establishing a budget and having an emergency fund goes hand-in-hand with planning for the future. It has to be done. You may start a family. You may want to travel. You may want to join a country club, etc. Therefore, you have to look into your future and come up with a plan. Your budget has to take your plan into account.

In coaching people, one of the things we do is come up with a plan. We call it a "smart plan." It is a measurable plan, and I'm not only talking about finances. It is a person's whole future. Where do they want to go? We paint a picture of the future, and then I move my clients into that picture. We do it with a plan. If you don't have a plan of your own, you are going to be part of somebody else's plan. You have to make a plan, and you have to stick to it. Execution is important. Accountability is also important. One of the things a coach does is help make you accountable. Think about the many plans that you have made, and why you have not followed through on those. It is because you are not accountable to anyone!

Let me tell you where a lot of people just don't get it on budgeting. You have to think about those little things. I love to smoke cigars, so I have to figure that in my budget. I spend about two hundred dollars a month on cigars. If I have not budgeted that, then that has to come from somewhere else. (Since I started this book, I quit smoking cigars. In effect, I gave myself a raise of two hundred dollars per month.) If you go by the boutique coffee shop every day and spend five dollars for a cup of coffee, you have to account for that. You have to account for the beer or cocktail after work. There is nothing wrong with drinking the designer coffee, having the beer after work, or smoking the cigars, so long as you have accounted for it in your budget.

As far as your business budget is concerned, you have to throw in marketing on top of all the other fixed expenses. Budgeting is important, both for the business and the home. You need to come up with a plan for both, make sure that those two plans integrate, and then stick with them.

One of the biggest problems that people need to overcome when dealing with finances is how they look to others. What do I mean by that? Well, many or most lawyers are very ego-driven, and that is part of their profession. The profession carries with it a certain amount of admiration, and people look to lawyers as business leaders and leaders in the community. But, there becomes a temptation to worry about how you look to others financially. It used to be called "keeping up with the Joneses."

I happen to drive a 2004 Lexus, so right now, in 2014; my Lexus is ten years old. It has 180,000 miles on it, and I'm perfectly happy with it. I want to confess to you, however, that in the early years of my life, before I realized a lot of these lessons that I'm passing on, I did have the two-seater Mercedes convertible and the 5-series BMW, both at one time. I only needed one car, but I had one for this event and one for the next. I'm sure I wanted that car, but there was that component in there about how I looked to others. Was it foolish? At the time, I had the money, and I didn't go in debt over it. I was settling or trying personal injury cases on a regular basis, and had a good income, so I could afford it. Would I do it again? Probably not. The problem arises when you can't afford it, but you do it because of outside pressure. If you can't afford it, you have to resist the temptations.

You have also got to be careful with your mortgage. One of the big mistakes young lawyers make is that they take out a mortgage the first year they start making a lot of money, so they can move into "that neighborhood"; the neighborhood where all the successful people live. What happens is, that income fluctuates. I guarantee you that emergencies are going to occur.

There was a young lawyer who worked for me years ago. He lived in a nice middle-class neighborhood. He had a wife and two kids, and he wanted to move because he was starting to make some good money. Rather than the three-bedroom house he lived in, he had his eye on a house that had five bedrooms and was located on the other side of town.

We talked about it, and I said, "You know of course, I have no control over whether or not you do it, but it looks to me like what you are doing is simply buying a bigger house for your wife and children to live in after you get divorced." Sure enough, he bought the bigger house for his wife and children to live in. The divorce followed right after. I don't know exactly why the divorce followed, but I would say that part of it was that he spent all of his time at work trying to make a mortgage payment.

Understanding credit cards is another important thing. Credit card living is very easy to do. You get this credit card, and you can run it up to twenty thousand dollars in no time and pay small amounts toward the balance. That is a loser's game. When you first start your practice, you are in transition and money is going to be tight. You might say, "Well, I can shop at the grocery store on a credit card." Sometimes that might be necessary, but you have to avoid the temptation of living above your means. It does not matter how you look to other people. It matters how good a lawyer you are. There are plenty of good lawyers who live well within their means.

We had a guy here in St. Charles County who probably hadn't bought a new suit in years. He was, however, one of the best lawyers in the county. He had a great practice, lived in a very modest house, and when he retired at age sixty-five, that was it. We never saw him again. Why? Because it wasn't important to him how he looked to others. He saved his money and he retired financially stable.

This is one of the most important aspects of living what I would call a "good life." A good life is not about how much money you make, or how much money you spend. A good life is about the quality of your life. It is about the time that you spend at work versus the time that you spend at home. It is about the time you spend enjoying this gift that you have called life. It is about enjoying your family and friends. If you are spending time at work because you like your work, you have found your niche and your purpose, and that is a wonderful thing. That is the way it should be. You can't be living your life at work in order to pay your bills to support your expensive habits, to pay off your credit cards, or pay your mortgage, which is bigger than it should be. You will find that your life is a lot better when you wake up in the morning, and the first thing you think about is how great your day is going to be, rather than the fact that more bills are coming in the mail.

With all the temptations to spend money that are around, financial responsibility is hard. As a lawyer, you get something in the mail every day, asking you to spend a couple more bucks. It is going to be another book. It is going to be another computer program. It is going to be another device of some sort. There is another seminar. There is always something.

I recently coached a lawyer who wanted to get in another practice area of law. He was fairly successful in what he was doing, but he wanted to explore expanding into this related field. A flyer for a seminar about his topic had reached his desk. We had a session over whether he should go to this seminar or not. The seminar was going to cost him 2,500 dollars, and he figured that with his traveling expenses, his hotel, and everything else, he would spend about another two thousand dollars, so the seminar would come to about 4,500 dollars total.

As his coach, I asked him to think about this in a global way. What was the fee potential of one of these cases? How many of these cases was he going to bring in? What other costs would he have if he got into this area of practice? How soon could he expect to bring in his first case? Were there other ways to start learning about this field of law that weren't as immediately cost intensive? We discussed a number of issues along those lines, and in the end, he decided not to go to that particular seminar. He told me recently that he had looked further into this area and decided it really wasn't something he would find interesting or remunerative.

Finances are important. They can kill you. They can ruin your happiness. They can tempt you to break the rules of ethics. They can ruin your family life. Therefore, pay attention to your finances, be financially independent, and restrain your spending.

Chapter 4
You Are the Brand

Three Step Process to Brand Mastery

As a lawyer, regardless of how big or how small your firm is, you are the brand. Look at some of the largest firms in America with these big partners who make almost unconscionable sums of money and crank out the work on a daily basis. The reason why they are in that position is because they are the brand to that particular client; whether it be a client like General Motors, AT&T, or any other big corporation, they have made themselves the brand to that client. That applies to those big guys as well as little guys like you and me. I am the brand.

How you relate to your clients and how your clients relate to you all depends on how you brand yourself. Who am I? As a lawyer, I'm a trial lawyer. I'm a good trial lawyer. I am known as a trial lawyer. I have a certain niche that I practice in, and that is what I do and what I am to my clients. When clients come here, they're looking for the Wayne Schoeneberg that they have heard about through their friends and family members. They are looking for that Wayne Schoeneberg. That is the line of thinking that you have to have.

There is a saying in the sales business called the ABCs of selling. The ABCs means, "Always Be Closing." For an attorney, whether you are in private practice or working for a firm, it should be ABM, "Always Be Marketing." Anybody who is in business and does not think that they are in marketing is doomed to fail. I said earlier that excellent service is what gets people to your door. That is true only to a limited extent because you have to get that first person to your door to do that. Again, you have to always be marketing.

There is another famous marketing myth that most believe to be true. "Build a better mousetrap and the world will beat a path to your door." That is the biggest lie in marketing. Because you can build the world's best mousetrap but if you do not let people know about it, they are not going to buy it.

Your type of practice determines your marketing strategy. Marketing for an associate in a big law firm is different than marketing for a sole practitioner. In either case, marketing is something that must always be happening. We will talk about sole practitioners in a minute. If you are an associate in a big law firm, your market is your partner, for the most part. They probably do not have you out trying to get new business. They have you down in the mine, digging coal. You need to market yourself to those partners.

There are many ways to market as a sole practitioner. You are going to be inundated by all sorts of marketing programs in the mail and on the Internet. I've read and studied many of them, and I've tried some of them. The first thing you need to know about marketing is that it is an excellent service that gets people to return to your door. That is not what gets them there in the first place. Knowing who you are is the first step.

The next thing you need to know is that you do not have to be on TV, but you do need to be seen. Here are some things that I would recommend to you about marketing.

I travel around the country on a regular basis, either as an attorney or a coach, or both. I'm always astounded when I ask lawyers I meet for a business card, and they get that look on their face that is sort of a "delay" look. I recognize it when I see it, and I've seen it a hundred or a thousand times. They start fumbling in their pockets and looking in their briefcases. They simply do not have a business card. OMG!

Everybody has to have a business card. Business cards are a must. It sounds rudimentary. I am shocked when people in business do not have a business card, but I still run into lawyers who do not have them. It is inexcusable not to have a business card. You are in business. They are called "business cards." Get it? You will never be so big, famous or successful that you do not need to have a business card.

Spend some time on your business cards. Go to your local printer. Ask them to design a card for you. That is what they do. They will be glad to work with you. There are tons of places on the Internet where you can design your own card, but think about shopping at your local businesses first.

If you can't find a suitable local source, Google "print business cards," and you will find any number of places that will help you get cards inexpensively. It does not have to be fancy, but it should be nice.

Before you get your business card printed, read the proof carefully. One time when I was going to be "Of

Counsel" to a law firm, the office manager brought me a box of a thousand business cards upon my arrival. She was proud of the fact they were so prepared. I looked at the cards and saw that the word "attorney" was misspelled. They had never bothered to proof the cards. Proof reading your material before it goes to the printer is that important.

When you get your card, get rid of it as quickly as you can. Give it to everyone you meet. That is the purpose of the business card. Set a goal. A good goal is to get your business card into the hands of at least three new people a week. Think of all the contacts that you are going to make if you do that for a year. I'm talking about just three new people. These can be three new businessmen. These can be three new clients. You can even go out on the street and talk to people, but set a goal.

Remember, it is "always be marketing." You should do something business-related in marketing every day for the first year of your practice, whether that is picking up the phone and calling somebody, emailing somebody, going out and shaking hands with a new person, or going to lunch with somebody. Do something business-related every business day. Give yourself Saturday and Sunday off. Five days a week for the first year of your practice take that business card and give it to people. Give it to the person at the grocery store. Give it to the person at the gas station. Give it to the person at the Laundromat, at the dry cleaners, or the person that you are standing next to.

I know it seems uncomfortable to many of you, but that is why you have the business card. That person might not need a lawyer right there and then. They might never need a lawyer. But just the fact that you have given out your business card is going to do a couple of things for you. First of all, it is going to spread your name. Secondly, it is going to make you more confident being who you are. I'm talking to the lawyers here. Remember the title of the book, *No Job, No Clients, No Problem*. You have to get out and spread the word about who you are. Make it your goal that every person in America should have your business card. Why not? You are here to practice law. You are here to do that thing that you want to do and that you have gone to school for. Remember that huge student loan debt? You got that so you could practice law. Start telling people you are a lawyer. Be proud about it. Be excited about it.

That is how I did it, and it will work for you too. That is how I started my coaching practice. I had been a lawyer for years. People knew that about me. But I had to get the message out that I was now a coach. I did it the same way I am telling you to do it. It works. You just have to work it.

Give extra business cards to your clients and tell them why. You are giving an extra card to them so that they can give it to a friend or family member who needs an attorney. Don't be shy about it because by the time they're your client, they like you. They want to help you, and it will make them feel important to have a lawyer. Therefore, give the client business cards. Give them out liberally and get them in everybody's hands. Now, please be aware of ethical rules here. Some jurisdictions have restrictions on giving business cards out to a third person and doing a mass handout. I think it is a dumb rule, but just beware that you do not violate any rules of conduct as you market your services. Remember the lesson from above: know the rules.

When I first started practicing law, there were very strict requirements on what was called advertising. Lawyers were not allowed to advertise at all. We could, however, have a business card with our name, attorney at law, our address, and our phone number, on it.

Since then, things have changed considerably. There are as many different types of lawyers out there as there are different opportunities for business cards. I consider my business card to be rather simple. It has the name of my law firm, Schoeneberg Tierney, with my name and telephone number underneath, and underneath that is my email address. On the other edge of the front face of the card is my address. Our logo and name is on there, and it says, "Trial Attorney." To me, that is sufficient to get the message across. If you have a web address, you might want to put it on the card. I try not to keep mine too crowded. I think that I have enough information for anybody to be able to contact me.

I believe that in today's electronic or digital world, if you have something on your card that will allow your current and potential clients to find your website, that should be enough. I do see many excellent business cards that have more on them; for example DWI law or traffic law, depending on what the person's niche is.

I do not believe that there should be writing on both sides of a lawyer's business card. The blank side is a good place to take a note, write an extra telephone number, write an extra email address, or something. You may even jot down the date of an appointment, so that if you meet somebody out somewhere, and they want to come see you,

you can write the date and time of the appointment and hand it to them so that they've got the reminder.

Just the other day, I handed out a new card to a guy at a gas station. I walked in, and he was the fellow behind the counter, so we chatted a little bit. He sees a lot of people every day, and somebody just might by chance say they need a lawyer, so I gave him my business card. When I came into his store, I wanted him to know that I am a lawyer. I want him to remember that.

Let me talk about something that stops more than just a few people from getting out of their comfort zone. That something is fear, especially the fear of not being good enough, and the thought that, "I'm not the right person for this." I help my clients deal with in this subject in our coaching all the time. Fear paralyzes us. It stops us from taking action. That is something that everybody faces to one degree or the next. Keep in mind, though, that rejection is something that you have to reach out and get. If you introduce yourself to someone as a lawyer, and they don't seem thrilled about you or the fact that you are a lawyer, forget about it. Move on to the next person.

I believe that there are no bad events in life. I believe that all things happen because they just happen. I'm not going to get into a long lecture on the "all things happen for the best" theory. Of course they do, but things just happen. They are neither good nor bad events. Rejection is something that you believe the other person is doing to you. Going out and not getting what you want, or having what you offer turned down, is simply an event, not a rejection.

If you are going to be in business, especially if you are going to be a lawyer, you are going to suffer what appears to be rejection all the time. Every time a client chooses a lawyer other than you, you could take that as a rejection. However, it just means that you were not the right lawyer for that person. Not everybody is the right lawyer for everybody. Not every attorney is the right lawyer for every client. You have to risk rejection, if you want to call it rejection, in order to make any progress.

If you stay within your comfort zone, you are never going to grow. You have to get out of your comfort zone. You have to feel some discomfort in what you are doing in order to move forward. Rejection is a self-imposed punishment, and there is no need to do that. If somebody says that you are not the person that they are looking for, that does not mean that you are bad, it just means that you weren't the person for the job. It is not a judgment. Being told "no" is not a judgment on you; it is just a decision that somebody else has made.

Now, let's switch gears and look at the importance of being involved in your community. It is not only extremely important, it is also extremely beneficial for an attorney to get involved in several different ways. Being an attorney gives you a certain opportunity to serve your community in many capacities. There is any number of service clubs that you can belong to that you can and should get involved in.

You should get involved for two reasons. The first reason is that I believe that you have a certain duty to your community to participate, to give back to your community, and you can do this by being a member of some service organization. Find out what service organization meets your needs. This goes back to purpose and niche. It does not do you or the organization any good to get involved in it if you don't believe in their purpose. If you don't believe in their goals, you are just going to give lip service to them, and it is going to come back and haunt you in the end. Then your reputation is going to be that you don't participate in any events and that you don't do your share. That is not going to help you at all. Look for a service organization to get involved with that you like and that you can be active in. It does not matter what it is, but is does matter that you give back to your community. That is one way to get involved in the community.

Another way to get involved in the community is through politics. Politics is a wonderful opportunity to meet people, get your name out, and make a difference in your community. Getting involved in politics does not mean that you have to run for office. You can get involved in city politics, state politics, or local politics. There are always areas for volunteers.

I've been involved in politics probably all of my adult life. I was Chairman of the Young Democrats when I was in college, and eventually I became Chairman of the Democrat Party here in St. Charles County. I ran for State Senate, unsuccessfully, I might add. Not once, but twice! It did not hurt my practice one bit. In fact I met hundreds of new people I never would have met. And these were people who got to know me. These were people who worked in my campaign. These were natural supporters. And I got all this publicity because people were willing to donate their money and time to advance my candidacy because I was willing to advance their cause.

It pleases people when I show up to help stuff envelopes, do a phone bank, or do something with the rank and file people. My clients are rank and file people. My clients are people who wear blue collars and go to work when they can find work. I like to work shoulder-to-shoulder with them. I learn from them. They pay me back with their loyalty to me. Sure, I could go out and make speeches, accompany candidates, go to the big events for each candidates, and pay the thousand dollars a plate for the dinner, but I do a service to my community, a service to my client, and a service to myself, by going out and volunteering to do the everyday things.

There are all sorts of ways to get involved in your community. Don't just shoot for just the ones that put you on top of the heap, especially if you are going to be in private practice. Start small. Before long you will be asked to step up and do more. But be a willing worker first. You'll get elevated to those higher jobs someday anyway. The cream rises to the top, and in time you will be asked to chair your share of boards and committees. You shouldn't go out and get involved in the community to make sure everybody knows you are a lawyer; go out and get involved in the community to make sure everybody knows that you are interested in your community. You will reap wonderful rewards doing that.

Getting involved in the community also involves getting to meet community leaders, and there are a couple of things that you really need to understand and appreciate about that. The leaders in each community are what I call centers of influence. These are people who shape opinions and policies large and small. You need to meet them. You do that by going to the various places the community leaders go.

These might be civic service organizations, political events, and charitable events. Meet these people. Keep in mind that they are interested in meeting people in the community who are up and coming. They want to meet people who are going to be successful. Sure, they may have their own lawyers already. That is okay. You should still meet them. Let them know that you exist, and after you have met them, go back to your office and write them a handwritten note telling them how happy you are to have met them.

A handwritten note is an incredible piece of marketing. Nobody writes handwritten notes any more, nobody but people who stand out. I have a good friend who is the

General Counsel, Partner, and all around an important person, in the largest Public relations firm in the world. Recently, my wife and I took her and her husband to dinner to celebrate an award she had received. I have known the woman and been good friends with her and her husband for almost thirty years. We have no pretense with each other. We are good friends. However, within a few days after the dinner, a handwritten thank you note appeared in my mailbox. She didn't have to do that. She did not have to even say, "Thank you" in person. We are friends. We were having dinner together to celebrate her victory. But she took the time to write the note. Do you see why she is successful?

Buy yourself some simple, inexpensive, blank fold-over cards at a stationary shop. After you have met somebody, go back to your office and write out a little note that just says, "Dear [Insert name here], It was a pleasure to meet you at [Insert place here] on [Insert time here]. I enjoyed speaking with you. Thanks for your time. Very truly yours..."

That person will get that handwritten note, open it, and I will bet you that it will stay on their desk for at least a day, because there is just something about this tangible handwritten note. A handwritten note trumps absolutely everything. People aren't accustomed to getting them. You should send them to new contacts you meet at networking functions. The idea is to stand out, and it is something that I can't beat the drum about enough. People don't do it; those who do it get results.

Marketing is about standing out from the rest. Be unique. Anhueser-Busch was recently involved in a big lawsuit in St. Louis. We all know them as one of the biggest breweries in the world. One of the corporate executives was testifying. He referred to the company as a marketing company. In other words, they make beer, sure, but they stand out by marketing their beer better than anybody else in the world.

Think of yourself as a marketing company. Be yourself. Don't be somebody else. Make yourself interesting to people. What is your hobby? Feel free to mention it. Find something about you that makes you stand out and then exploit that. I am sure there is something about you that is interesting or unique

Ask about other people's hobbies as well. Ask people about themselves. People love to talk about themselves. When the conversation is over, and you have listened to all they have to say, they will think you are the best conversationalist in the world.

The last thing I want to suggest on marketing, and I can't tell you how important this is, is to start keeping a client list. Use that list to keep in touch with your clients. Send a birthday card to each client every year. Send them a Christmas card. I have experienced clients coming into my office with a new case without having seen me for seventeen years. When we sat down to discuss the case, they mentioned that they got a Christmas card from me every year. Believe me, it is worth it. Keep in touch with your clients. They are a gold mine. They are your best source of new business.

I will probably never retire. I enjoy practicing law, I enjoy coaching, and I get paid to do what I enjoy. I now represent grandchildren of clients that I started representing years and years ago. That legacy is important to me, not only because it keeps the practice going, it is also very gratifying.

Remember that you always have to be marketing. Everything is a marketing event. With every person you meet, there is an opportunity for a marketing event, but you don't have to make it look like a marketing event. Take interest in people. When you meet somebody and strike up a conversation, I will tell you that the most important person in the world is that make them feel that you feel that way about them, too. It really isn't much to ask, is it? Ask questions about them, rather than talking about yourself. Remember that you have given them a business card. Now, give them the gift of listening to what they have to say. They're going to remember you because you had taken an interest in them.

There are always ads on television for lawyer services. There is no way you are going to be able to fight those, unless you have some huge budget. This is a much better method of marketing. You get your clients marketing for you because you bring them in, and you do a good job for them. When you go out and meet these people one-on-one, remember that they're important. Remember that though they might not need a lawyer then, when they or a family member of theirs needs a lawyer, you want them to dig in their wallets and say, "Hey, I talked to this man or this woman and they are really smart. They are nice. They are pleasurable. They are good people, and you should call them." Set your goal to do it every day. Though it is hard sometimes, it will make you successful.

I am not going to say much about Social Media. That is a subject that you can Google until your fingers bleed. Facebook, Twitter, Instagram, and whatever may come on the market before this book is published all have their place. Know about them and use them. Learn about them. Use them to keep your name in front of your friends, clients and family members. But even in this day of digital marketing nothing succeeds like personal contact.

Chapter 5

There is No 'I' in Team (Teach, Evaluate, Advise, Motivate)

Can You Create a Culture That Clicks?

Employees are an important element of any law office, and it has been my experience that attorneys don't always recognize the importance of the people in the front office, the people who are in the typing pool, or the people who answer the phone. However, they are a part of your team. They are a part of your business and a part of who you are.

One of the first things that you have to do when you hire an employee is look for somebody who is going to fit in with the rest of your team. Find somebody who is interested in what they do and what your firm does. Then make them know that they are part of the team. I use the term "team," and I'm going to break that into an acronym that will help you understand some key elements in creating a great work culture.

The first part is the "T": "Teach." You hire a new employee and they come into the office. So often I see lawyers who just sit their employee down at the desk and tell them to get started. That is unfair to the employee, and subsequently it will come back to haunt you. The first thing you have to do is teach your employee how to do their job. Let them know what is expected of them. I bring them in and give them a briefing about what the job entails. I take them through the various elements of the job and we have a procedures manual, which we've compiled over the years, that I give them. This shows them how to handle everything from a traffic ticket to a murder case, at least from their perspective. I go over that manual with them while telling them what I expect from them. I also tell them that I want them to ask me if they do not know or are unsure of how to do something. I will answer their questions as many times as they ask. I would rather have an employee ask me how to do something than do it wrong and cause some problem for a client.

It is not fair to sit an employee at a desk and have them try to intuit what you want. It takes some time, but it is an investment. It is an investment in that employee who is an asset to your company. Replacing employees is time-consuming and expensive. Every time you bring in a new employee, there is going to be a learning curve. That is going to cost you money. You might not realize that, but it does.

Do not hold back on the specifics. Tell them how to answer the phone, how to route messages or take messages, and show them how to make appointments for you. Tell them what an appointment is going to entail; for instance, an appointment for a new client may last an hour or more, whereas an appointment for an existing client may only take a half hour. Explain it to them. You want them to be the best employee they can be, don't you? Well, give them a hand.

You want your employees to know those sorts of things, so that when they're doing a simple task like making an appointment for you, they understand what you are going to be doing. Teach them how to deal with the clerks in the courts. Show them how cases progress. Show them what the progression is on a traffic ticket. Show them what the progression is on a misdemeanor. Show them what the progression is on a domestic case, or if you are doing transactional work, let them know what's going to be involved. Tell them why a certain document has to have certain components. Teach them everything they need to know. It is absolutely critical for their ability to be part of the team to know what you expect from them. If they know what you expect from them, they will give that to you.

If they do not know, they are going to be frustrated. You have to understand that when you have these employees and you are their boss, they have a certain amount of apprehension every day when they come to work as to whether or not they're performing up to your expectations. This leads me up to the second part of the word "team."

The second part of "team" is "E": "Evaluate" their performance. Set aside a few moments each week and look at each employee's work. This is part of your product. This will only take a small part of your time. Did this employee have any problems completing their assigned tasks? How would you know that? You would ask them. That's right, communicate with your employees. They are helping you be successful. Most of the time, the general public never learns about the hard work and dedication of the law firm's employees. The awards and recognition go to the attorneys. But the employees make it all possible, so evaluate their performance.

Did you notice anything especially good or bad about an employee's performance? Make note of it. Let them know about the good performance as often as the poor performance. With your careful supervision and guidance, you should soon have very few negatives to point out. Your employees, whether they are attorneys or non-legal support staff, are the shoulders you are standing upon. They will lift you high if you treat them right. They will let you fall if you don't. Evaluate their work. They want to know.

Now we get down to the "A" in "team": "Advise" your employees how they are doing. Employees want to know how they are doing, and they deserve to know how they are doing. If you have a complaint about an employee's performance, you need to discuss that with him or her. You can't just go back to your office and scratch your head and wonder why they don't get it.

A lawyer and I were talking about an employee who didn't seem to do everything the way the lawyer thought she should. He was constantly complaining about her not being able to meet his rather strict standards. I pointed out that if this legal secretary were able to perform like a lawyer, she wouldn't be a legal assistant. She'd be doing his job.

An important part of supervising an employee is to let them know when they're doing a good job. Employees want to be praised for their good work and they deserve to be. You can't just take an employee and criticize their work. You have to start by telling them the things that they're doing right. You have to acknowledge when they're doing things right, so that they will be encouraged and secure. An insecure employee starts looking for another job. An employee who is not getting any feedback wonders how they're doing. You have to take the human element into account here.

Don't just put an employee in their chair behind their desk and let them hang out there wondering how they're doing. Schedule a review with them. Quarterly will be enough in most cases. Put it on the calendar so the employee and you both know it will take place. Each quarter, bring them in, sit them down, and tell them the good things they're doing as well as the things that they can improve on. They want to know that, but you have to do that in a professional manner. Being a manager, being an employer, being a boss, is a special job, a special position. These people rely on you for their employment, and they are dedicated to you, but you have to give them feedback. You have to let them know how they're doing. It is absolutely important to them. Again, if they're doing well, tell them that they are.

Lastly, motivate your employees. The "M" in team is: "Motivate!" How do you that? Well, there are a number of ways to motive employees. One is through the reviews we already discussed. The other, of course, is pay. Pay is always an issue. Lawyers all want to hire the cheapest employee that they can because of cash flow. That usually is not the best answer. If you get the right employee, the right legal assistant, he or she makes you money. They'll free your time up to practice law, which is the whole purpose of having employees. That is their purpose in your law firm. Think about it. You can do everything that your employee does; you can type, you can file, you can answer the phone. They are doing those things for you so that you can practice law.

How do you motivate your employees? You motive them with praise. You motivate them by letting them know how important they are to the team. Let them know that. Show them how they fit into the process. Tell them how critical it is to the success of the firm that they are successful in their job. After all, it is the truth. Let them see how important they are, how important that initial client contact is, how important the follow-up is, and how important it is for them to be communicating with the courts. Everything they do is important or you wouldn't have them there. If you have non-critical employees, that is on you as a manager. You cannot afford to have people you don't need.

There is nothing wrong with occasionally doing something special for your staff. How about sending them on a trip for a weekend? You know that trip is going to stick in their minds. Send them to a place a hundred miles away and pick up their hotel bill and their expenses. What's that going to cost you – five hundred dollars? You will get those five hundred dollars back many, many times. I have a friend who sends his secretary on a cruise once a year. She has been with him for thirty-four years. He has made that money back over and over again.

Motivating your employees is important. To do it well, you have to find out what they want and what motivates them. It takes time to be an employer. It takes time to have a good staff. You have to devote that time and develop those skills to become a good boss. I coach people on leadership skills all the time. Leadership is part of being a good boss. Being a good leader is not something that just happens. You have to develop your skills and then work at keeping them sharp. In my coaching business, I use what is called the Energy Leadership Development System.™

Being a good boss is important, and your employees will be proud of you. They will be proud to work for you. They will be your emissaries in the community. They'll get you business. That is why you need to teach, evaluate, advise, and motivate – TEAM.

Every individual has a different motivation, a different purpose, and a different goal. The little things are important. Remembering an employee's birthday is certainly a nice thing, but there are circumstances where just doing something simple, like bringing them a dessert when you come back from lunch, giving them a gift card for their favorite place, or even a Starbucks card, just something to let them know that you are interested in them and you are rewarding them for doing a good job.

Other motivations can be doing something for their family, like remember their kids' birthdays. They are not just employees, they are human beings. They are people who have the same wants, desires, hopes, and fears that you do. Make them a part of your life. They are part of your professional life. Make them feel that way. Of course some people are just motivated by money. If that is what they want, make sure you recognize it.

I had a secretary who I would always give a Christmas gift to. She had worked with me for a long time, and I knew about her home situation, which was not particularly good. She had a boyfriend who was not very nice to her. We sat down and I said, "Look, it's Christmas time. I will give you a cash bonus if you want a cash bonus. What would you really like to have?" She replied, "Well, what I'd really like to have is an iPad, because if you give me a cash bonus, I put it into my account and my boyfriend will spend it." So I bought her an iPad instead for Christmas.

It is a question of knowing your individuals and talking with them. It goes back to finding out that they are and treating them like people. Everybody is going to have a different motivation, a different reason for coming to work. Some are motivated by acknowledgement, some are motivated by money, and some are just motivated by having a job. It is part of the process to learn who they are, treat them like you would want to be treated, and do the little things for them. Remember their birthdays, their kids' birthdays, and their anniversaries. Give them a gift certificate to a nice restaurant for their anniversary. It is the little things that motivate people. It is the little things that keep them loyal to you. It is the little things that help them feel like a part of your life and a part of your team, and make them feel secure. Being secure is what an employee wants most of all. They want to know that they are appreciated and they want to know that their job is not on the line every day.

The workplace lends itself to a lot of different issues. One of the issues is the relationship between the boss and the employees. In a situation where you are working with somebody every day for long hours, a relationship can start to develop without you recognizing it until it has gone too far. That could be a relationship between the boss and the staff, the boss and a co-worker, or just co-workers. Many times, those relationships cross a line. They start by going out for a drink after work or going to lunch together. It starts slowly. It starts by beginning a relationship that is not solely worker-to-worker, and then it slowly works its way into something more. Suddenly it is romantic or sexual.

Clearly, that is an absolute prohibition. It is something that has to be guarded against constantly. Lawyers are in a position of power, and certain people are attracted to this power. They find it intoxicating. Employees can become so admiring or enamored of the lawyer in the office, that suddenly they find themselves romantically attracted. You occupy a position of power and influence. You are spending a lot of time in the office with this person whom you find pleasant and fun to be around, and it is flattering that this person thinks that you are so wonderful and that you can do no wrong.

The next step is to become romantically involved. There might be a casual touch, a brush of the shoulder, and hands touching. The next thing you know, you are in a relationship that you shouldn't be in. This applies whether you are married or not. Having a romantic or sexual relationship with an employee or co-worker is just dangerous. Not only is it dangerous, it is just something you absolutely want to avoid at any expense.

First of all, it is going to end poorly, there is no question about that. As soon as you become romantically or sexually involved with an employee, their work production goes down, and they expect special favors and special treatment. Consequently, your business suffers. After it becomes known in the community, your reputation suffers. Nobody wants to do business with somebody who is sexually involved with his or her secretary, his or her co-workers, or their boss. It just does not make sense.

There can also be situations where lawyers who work in the same office and are equals, become romantically involved. Is that a good idea? Probably not. I have a friend who went to another state and worked for a big law firm. She was an associate, and she got involved with one of the partners. They kept it secret for a long time, and nobody found out about it for probably two years. Then it came up in a partnership meeting, and not only did the associate lose her job, but the partner lost his job because they couldn't fire the associate for violating the rules without terminating the partner. Two great careers in a great law firm got ruined over this one romantic relationship. It just does not pay.

If a person's work begins to suffer because of a romantic involvement in the office, and you want to replace them, then you are in a box you can't get out of. You can't fire them, because if you do, you'll end up with a lawsuit on your hands. I can't stress enough how dangerous these matters are, and how important it is that you don't get involved with an employee.

Also, stay out of your employees' personal lives. You are going to learn about it anyway, but do not start giving advice to them as to what they should do in their personal lives. It is none of your business. It is their business. Obviously, if their personal life starts to affect their work performance, you have to deal with that, but you can't deal with that by micromanaging their personal life. You have to deal with that professionally as to how it affects your law firm, and if you are unable to rehabilitate them and get them back to working at full strength, then you have to let them go. If you have been giving them advice as to what to do in their personal life, and then you want to fire them for mistakes they've made in that area, you have a certain liability. Therefore, treat your employees professionally. Hold them at arms' length. Do not become romantically involved with them. Do not become sexually involved with them. Stay out of their personal lives.

Earlier, we talked about behaving as though someone is watching you. There are times when you have to bring an employee into your office and close the door, if only for confidentiality purposes, or because you are dealing with certain issues in a lawsuit. Clearly, if you are in a one-lawyer office and you have one secretary, there is no reason to come in and close the door.

But you are going to find yourself in situations where that employee of the opposite sex or even of the same sex, depending on your sexual orientation, is there alone at the office with you. Then you have to conduct yourself as though someone is watching you. You have to keep that in mind. Gauge every one of your actions by what someone else think of what you are doing. If you have an office with many employees, and there is no reason to close the door, then don't do it. There is no reason to be isolated from everybody else.

There are certain situations where an employee might take advantage of that regardless of what you have or have not done. They might make an allegation that you have done something that is inappropriate. Again, that depends upon the size of your law firm and your business. It is difficult sometimes to not be in a situation where you are one-on-one with other employees, especially when you have a small law firm. If you establish the rules early on, and there is no question about your intent to remain aloof from that person, you are on solid ground. Should an employee be making advances to you, or if an employee did something that would be considered inappropriate, they need to be told about that at that particular moment. You cannot discipline an employee effectively for doing something that is considered inappropriate if you have engaged in the same conduct.

Sometimes, when I have been in law firms to take depositions, I have heard lawyers make comments to secretaries about how they look on a certain day, a dress they have on, or the clothes they wear. I find that totally inappropriate.

There has to be a professional and distant relationship between the lawyers and the employees, and it has to exist at all times. You have to be vigilant about it. There are going to be times where it is a temptation to tell an off-color joke, use sexual innuendo at an event, or snicker about the titillating facts of a lawsuit. It is something about which you must be constantly vigilant. Make sure that there is no room for doubt as to your professional demeanor in a situation.

To sum up, remember that your employees are people. They have this job because they need this job. They want this job. They applied for it. You wanted them because you hired them. Treat them like people. Treat them with respect. Make them part of the team. Let them know how important they are. Pay them well and validate them. Treat them like professionals, and they will treat you like a professional and help your business grow.

Chapter 6
Family First

The Best Practice there is

There is an old saying that, "the law is a jealous mistress," and the saying is very true. Lawyers come out of law school all fired up to practice law. They're excited, as they should be. They want an opportunity to put their skills into action and they dive into their job. New associates in big firms take jobs that require them to bill outrageous numbers of hours each year and the job consumes them. That is an area of the practice that I should write an entire book about. I think some big law firms are almost defrauding their big corporate clients. If you are not working in a big law firm, you are trying to start your own practice, and that takes a lot of time too.

Many of these lawyers have spouses. Some have spouses and children. You have to remember that being a good lawyer is not as important as being a good family member. Let me say that again so there is no mistake: Being a good lawyer is not as important as being a good family member. Your family should be your first priority. It is not easy to balance your obligations to your profession and your family, especially when you are starting out. You feel consumed with building your practice. However, if you take the attitude that you will work your family in and around your practice, you are putting the cart before the horse. Family obligations should come first.

There are times when the demands of the practice are such that you have to be away from your family for long periods of time. These might be the long days that you have to put in. For example, I called my dad one night. It was 10:00 at night, and I said:

Dad, this morning I had to be in court downtown in St. Louis at 8:00, and from there I went to court in St. Louis County. There I was until about Noon, and then I had to go to court in St. Charles County, and I was there until about 4:00. Now I'm at a City Council meeting, and it's 10:00 at night. I really called you just to thank you for that great advice about getting a law degree and working for myself.

Of course, that was his advice. He had worked for someone else all his adult life. He had been an employee and he had some pretty rotten bosses. He wanted to save me from that and always encouraged me to strike out on my own. I did and am happy to this day that I did. But in the early years, I put in entirely too much time with my mistress "the law" and not enough with those I chose to be members of my family.

There are days when you are going to be gone all day! That is understandable, and it happens. You might even be out of town on a case. Sometimes it is unavoidable. However, if you consistently make the effort to make your family the first priority, you are going to find that you are happier and that you are just as good at being an attorney, maybe even better.

I look at it this way; your spouse made a commitment to you. You and your spouse stood in front of a bunch of your friends and family members, and you took an oath. Maybe you wrote your own vows that you promised to love and care for one another. You recited that oath as a verbal expression of your love and devotion. Your spouse depends on you, not only for your economic input, but also to be a friend. They are depending on you for those intimate, gentle moments when he or she needs that special person to be there for them, and you made a commitment to do that. Now, you took an oath to practice law too, and I understand that, but it is easy to get consumed with the practice of law. Suddenly, you might feel you have to put your spouse in second place. You do not have to do that, but you do it anyway. Then, all of a sudden, you look around and ask why your spouse seems so distant.

Let me tell you a story. Many years ago, I was married to a wonderful girl who was very committed to me and to our marriage. She had a son from a previous marriage who lived with us, and we were a great family. I was young though, and very committed to the practice of law. The law and building that law practice became everything to me. It seemed like my wife and I argued frequently over the fact that I spent too much time at work. My response was of course to show her the beautiful house we lived in, the great cars we drove, and all of the fine clothes we wore, and I pointed out to her that she had everything she could desire financially. It took me years and a failed marriage to realize that really wasn't what she wanted. She wanted me to spend more time with her. She wanted the family she thought we formed together. Of course, I wanted to spend my time practicing law because that gave me a great thrill.

One Christmas, she had her family over to our house for a Christmas dinner celebration. Her mother, her grandparents, her brother, and her sister, were there, and there was a warm, fun family gathering. We were just getting ready to distribute gifts when the phone rang. The alarm had gone off at our office, and I was the third person on the list of people to be called. Apparently, the first two either didn't answer the phone, or just passed it off to me. There were other people on the list, and I could have excused myself and passed it on to the next person, but I felt it was my responsibility to take care of it, so I didn't pass it off. My wife's disappointment was palpable when I told her that I had to leave the family gathering to go to the office to see whether or not there had been an actual break-in, or if it was just a false alarm.

This was part of her family Christmas. She had made a wonderful meal, and had planned a great evening together with her family. She was really looking forward to the entire event. It was her opportunity to show off her house and her new family. Instead, I chose to leave and drive to the office to see about the alarm.

As I look back on this, do I regret it? Yes. Was it the right thing to do? No, it was not the right thing to do, but I was consumed with the practice of law, being a lawyer, and being important. I put that priority ahead of my family, and it is just one of the many times that I have put my obligation to my business ahead of my obligations to my family. That marriage ended in divorce.

If there is a happy note to this story, it is that I ran into her son many years later. We have become rather close. He refers to me as "dad," and he's grown up to be a proud father of three boys himself. He is happily married and he is successful in his career. I hope he learned a few good lessons from me in the time I was married to his mother. This was a situation, though, where I as a young lawyer was so consumed with practicing law, that I totally ignored the simple things that this woman wanted. It was simple. She wanted some quality time and attention from me.

Let's talk about children. Your children need you more than your clients need you. Your clients are important, yes, but you brought these children into the world. It was your decision to have them. You owe them your time and your attention. Sometimes it seems like they are demanding. They are. They have a right to be. It is your duty to spend quality time with your children. It is more important to be a good parent than it is a good lawyer.

I am coaching a lawyer right now who contacted me about helping him simplify his practice. That was his goal when we started. I asked him what he meant by that. He was not clear about it at first. We worked on his procedures. We worked on his forms. We worked on his calendar. Eventually he told me that he wanted to simplify his practice so he could spend more time with his children. That is a good goal. I asked him whether he would be willing to schedule time with his children and put it on his calendar? By doing that, as calculated, as it may seem, he made them a priority.

He came up with a plan. He started by turning his cell phone off at five o'clock on Tuesdays and Thursdays and leaving it off until the next morning. Then he would go home and do something with his kids. It could be as simple as taking a walk, playing catch, or helping with homework. I thought he was going to crawl out of his skin the first week. But when he realized he did not miss any important business opportunities by doing this, he got more comfortable.

Sure, he missed those calls his clients had become accustomed to making to him in the evenings, but he discovered that those same things could be covered during business hours. What he realized was that he was putting his clients' wants above those of his children.

Suddenly, he found himself spending two nights a week with his cell phone turned off, simply spending time with his children. Did his work suffer? No. His mistake had been making the office work a priority and trying to fit his children in around that. Once he saw that he could make his kids a priority by putting them on a calendar, he was able to find time for them. Although it seems rather rigid, what he discovered was that he did have time for the family once they became a priority, and he still had time to get his law work done.

Whether you are a husband and a father, or a wife and a mother, you might sometimes feel that bringing home an income is what you are there for. If you stop and listen to your kids and your spouse, you will learn that that isn't what is really important to them. Your spouse married you for better or worse, and what they want from you is your time, your attention, your love, and your affection.

The lawyer I was just talking about would get to the office at 6:00 in the morning, and he'd stay until 10:00 at night. What was clear to me was that he was getting a lot of satisfaction from his practice that he wasn't getting at home. The reason he wasn't getting satisfaction at home, was because he wasn't contributing anything but money.

He wasn't getting any positive feedback at home because he wasn't putting anything into his family other than money.

Your spouse wants quality time with you. That is why they married you. They didn't marry you to watch you practice law. Your kids don't want to watch you practice law either. They want you to hold them, hug them, take them to soccer practice, watch them in their swim meets, have dinner with them, go to their ballet recitals, and to share your experiences with them. The role of a parent is extremely important. It is the most important job that you will have. It is far more important than anything you will ever do as a lawyer. Make your family a priority. Doing that will pay you back in dividends much greater than you are ever going to get from practicing law. I know you want money and success. Believe me on this, you will feel more successful by having a good, solid, stable family life than you ever will by accumulating large sums of money.

Bringing home money is one thing, buying things is another. I used to spend way too much time at the office. I told my wife (ex-wife) that I did that so she could have nice things. It seemed simple to me. I was obviously getting more satisfaction at the office than I was at home. The answer to the question "why?" could take up an entire chapter. But I was clearly not paying enough attention to my family obligations and responsibilities. I thought that I could buy peace with my wife by buying her things. What she really wanted was somebody to love and appreciate her. She wanted somebody to help her in her tough times. She wanted somebody to listen to her and talk to her. I just didn't have time. Hey, I was practicing law and bringing home money. I was spending all my time taking care of me!

One of the problems that lawyers have is turning off their lawyer-like ways once they get home. Lawyers spend a lot of time solving other people's problems. They know how to do it. It is a very linear and logical process. The problem they have is that once they get home, they can't quit being a lawyer.

Once they get home, their problems are not necessarily linear and logical. For instance, lawyers don't like long stories. They want to get to the point. When clients come into the office, they will tell you in an hour what they could have told you in five minutes. Lay people want to tell a story. Your spouse is probably not a lawyer. They do not want you to interview them about their day. They want to tell you about their day. They will generally do it in a long, circuitous way. They want you to take the time to listen to them. You want to get to the end of the story. You are a lawyer. You want to solve the problem. The thing you need to accept is that most of the time there is not a problem that needs to be solved. There is only a person who wants to share their day with you. Listen!

Another thing you must not do is put your spouse or your children on the witness stand. You know what I mean. Lawyers do it all the time. Even lawyers who do not do trial work do it. Keep in mind that a discussion is not like a cross-examination. I have been accused more than once in my past marriages of cross-examining my wife while I simply thought I was engaging in a conversation. It was not something I tried to do, or did consciously. It came naturally to me. But your house isn't a courtroom.

Although you are in control of your environment when you are at the office, it is not going to be like that at home. Get used to it. When you come home, you have to be a spouse and a parent first. Leave the lawyer at the office. You are in an adversarial profession, even if you are in transactional work. But the folks at home are not interested in being treated like adversaries. They want to be treated like your family. They deserve it.

There are going to be times when you and your spouse don't get along. That is perfectly natural. Two people can't live in perfect harmony. You have to accept that as a fact. Still, you don't have to let it be destructive. I, again, suffered from this in my early years, where my wife and I would get into an argument, and we wouldn't resolve it. It would still be going on when I left for work because I had to win the argument or it wasn't over. I would spend a great portion of that day distracted by the argument that was waiting for me when I got home. I would be thinking about that and dealing with that, rather than tending the business at hand.

When you are at the office, your job is to tend to the law business, the interests of your clients. Do not let your problems at home drag on. Do not bring them to the office with you. Solve them immediately. If you have to stay up half the night talking it out, talk it out. If you have problems at home, and you don't resolve them immediately, they are going to spill over into your work performance. You are going to be distracted. You will make mistakes. You will be unpleasant to be around. Your clients will notice, your co-workers will notice, and it will hurt you in the long run.

If you are lucky, and if you put in the effort, your family is going to be with you for the rest of your life. You may want to practice law for the rest of your life. Great! Through the course of your life, you will get much more fulfillment from your family than you do from practicing law. I promise you that.

Remember, when you get in an argument with your spouse, there are two sides. Lawyers always want to believe that they are right. That is their nature. They always find a way to advance their side of the argument. They are always advocating positions for their clients. When they get involved in a confrontation at home, they want to advocate their position as correct. Here is the harsh truth: you are not always right! Deal with it. You have to listen to what your spouse and your children have to say. They have a point of view that needs to be considered. You do not have to win every time.

As a matter of fact, no one has to win and no one has to lose. What you need to do is try and fashion a situation in which everybody wins. After all, you are an intelligent, educated individual. You would bend over backwards to come up with a suitable solution for a problem for your client. Suddenly, when you are faced with a situation where you have some skin in the game, you begin to take it personally. You have to do for your family what you would do for your clients. You have to bend over backwards to come up with a suitable solution for all concerned. Your family depends on you. They depend on you for leadership. They depend on you for support. I do not mean just economic support. They need emotional support as well. They look to you for wisdom and for you to lead. You are a leader. You are an educated professional. You have been trained to help your clients. Use those same skills at home. Remember, if you have problems at home that are unresolved, you are going to have problems at work.

I suspect that most couples argue more about finances than anything else. If you are married or in a relationship, it is an equal partnership. You may be out making all of the money or the "big money." That does not matter. It is an equal partnership. You made a commitment to your partner, and he or she has made a commitment to you. That commitment means sharing everything.

There are going to be ups and downs, good times and bad times. There are going to be times of riches and times of austerity. I have heard too many people complain about their spouse's spending habits. Why does that happen? Why is one partner spending too much? No spouse wants to spend themselves or the family into bankruptcy. Nobody in his or her right mind intentionally does that. If you, as the provider, do not openly and honestly discuss your finances with your spouse or your partner, they might not understand it when you complain about their spending. When you get upset with your wife for buying a new purse or a pair of shoes that you don't think are necessary, or you are mad at your husband for buying a new shotgun that you don't think is necessary, suddenly, it is a big issue. If you have an honest and open discussion about your finances and an understanding that you are both in it together, as equals, those issues won't come up.

This comes back to having a budget. Sit down with your spouse, discuss what money is coming in and how it is to be spent, and be realistic. Be considerate. Don't establish a budget that is heavily weighted on the things you want without considering your spouse's needs.

When I used to handle divorces, I was always surprised at how people would propose to divide their property. I was just as surprised as to how they accumulated the property.

In many instances, there were all sorts of toys that had been accumulated by the men in the marriages. There were four-wheelers, guns, fishing equipment, and boats, but hardly ever any discretionary purchases for the wife. When it came time for the divorce, I would explain that the property had to be divided equitably. That didn't go over too well. Why? Because that meant the husband was going to have to give up some of "his" things to make the equation balance. He would say that, "she can't have my boat, my guns, and my four wheelers." Of course there wouldn't really be anything left for her. "Well, she can have the children's furniture," they would say.

You have to have an open and honest discussion with your spouse, and you have to constantly remember that you are equal partners in your relationship. If you do not consider yourself to be equals, then it is you who are wrong. Deal with it. You have to let your significant other know where the money is coming from. You have to agree on how it will be spent. Your spouse may have different needs or wants than you do. Your spouse may want to remodel the kitchen. You may think it is unnecessary. Sit down and discuss it, talk about it. Make a joint decision about these things.

As I discussed earlier in this book, saving is a necessity. How much you save and how you go about it is another area that needs to be discussed and agreed upon. If you come to an agreement about savings, you can work as a team to encourage one another to stick to the plan. Too often a savings plan is conceived but not carried out. One of the benefits of coaching is that the coach helps people be accountable. You and your spouse can work together to reach your savings goal. However, you cannot do it if both of you are not on the same page. Discuss the options and come up with a plan. Then do it.

You do that through open and honest communication on a regular basis. If you are the wage earner, it is not "your" money. It belongs to both of you. If your spouse is a stay-at-home spouse, whether a mom or a dad, that money you are earning belongs to both of you. You have to treat your spouse with respect financially and make them a partner, an equal partner.

If you have made the decision to have a family, you have made a commitment to everybody in that family that you will treat them as your first priority. You have to constantly keep that in mind. Evaluate your performance in that respect because when you get right down to it family is the most important thing in your life. You may think that practicing law or being a good lawyer is the most important thing in your life. It is not. Do not be deceived. Do not fall prey to they sultry mistress of the "law." If you have made the decision to have a family, you should respect that as the most important commitment you have made.

Chapter 7
Courting Clients

What is More Important – Client Value or Client Connection?

Now, turn your attention to how you treat your clients. I can't say enough about courting clients. Clients are the most important assets in your business. They are the reason you are in business. Without clients you would not be able practice law.

I frequently walk into rooms with groups of lawyers and hear them saying, "if it weren't for the client, practicing law would be okay," and everybody chuckles. Even though this is meant as a joke, the thought has a pervasive influence. Thinking that way about clients, even as a joke, influences your feelings about them. Clients are not the enemy. Clients are your friends. From time to time, I see lawyers frown, make a face, and run their hands through their hair as though it is an annoyance, when clients call. These people are your friends and you are their friend. Act like it.

Remember that most of the time clients come to you in a time of trouble. Nobody comes to a lawyer when they are having a good time. People do not call attorneys because everything is running smoothly in their lives. They come to a lawyer because they are in some state of concern or need. They might just need a simple will, or it might be something much more serious. It could be a family law case, a criminal case, personal injury case, or a real estate transaction. These people come to you for your help. Without them you would be nothing as a lawyer. These are the people that are giving you the opportunity to use the skills that you went to law school to learn. These are the people who are giving you the opportunity to put your skills into action. Without them you'd be like a bell without a clapper. From a business perspective, these assets should be treated like gold. Every client you get has the potential to make you very successful and very rich. There is no such thing as a small client, only small lawyers. Never value the worth of a client by the size of the fee.

Okay, time for another story. When I first started practicing law, I came out of law school with no job and no clients. I was just like the title of this book. I had a goal, though. In fact, I had a number of goals. Some were very specific. Some were more general. One was to be successful. I was happy to get any case that I could when I first started. It did not matter how big the fee was. It was an opportunity to build my practice one client at a time.

There was a certain man who came to my office one time and asked me to represent him on a collection case. He was being sued for a couple of hundred dollars and he admitted he owed the money. At first I thought, "Well, there is nothing I could really do for him. I couldn't charge him much money for a two hundred dollar lawsuit." However, I took his case. If he did not use me as his lawyer, he would us somebody else. I went to law school to be a lawyer. This guy had a case. I had more time on my hands than money, and this guy was a pretty nice man. He was just on hard times. Heck, I was not that far away from being broke, too. So maybe I just felt sorry for him. I took his case. I worked something out with the collection lawyer. The man entered into a payment program and his debt was paid off. Everybody won.

It wasn't long before he came back with a very similar lawsuit. Over the course of the next two years, I probably represented him half a dozen times on small collection matters. Each time, I could just charge him a nominal amount of money. He appreciated that and became a regular client. I was happy to be of service. I just wanted clients at that point, and I was glad to have him as one. I was always excited to see him, even if I only made twenty-five dollars or fifty dollars on each case. I knew that if I gave him good service, he'd tell his friends. They might have something more serious and more profitable.

One weekend, I had been out of town to a legal seminar. I did not take a real vacation for years when I was young. I would go to seminars in nice locations and use that as my vacation. That way I could get my continuing legal education hours, have some time away from the office, and also make contacts with other attorneys.

When I got home after this weekend, there was a message on my answering machine. The man who I had represented on all of the little collection cases was asking if I would represent him on a new case. It seems that his son was killed that weekend in a railroad crossing accident. That case brought my first six-figure fee.

Another time I represented a young man in a DWI case. I was lucky enough to get him acquitted. At the end of the case, he still owed me a hundred dollars. I didn't think I would ever collect it, and I wasn't about to chase him down for a hundred dollars. I did not want to make an enemy out of a guy who had given me an opportunity to handle his case. So we maintained a good relationship when we parted.

One day, his mother called me. She said, "Tim knows that he still owes you a hundred dollars. He is really sorry about not paying you. He needs your help. Would it be okay if I brought you the money he owes, and you took his case? He really wants you to represent him."

Tim had been horribly burned in a fire at his mobile home. A fitting had come loose and there was an LP gas explosion. I do not know if you know this. LP gas is odorless and colorless. It is also heavier than air. When it leaks out of a loose fitting, it sinks to the floor. A chemical is added to LP gas to give it that nasty smell. The problem is that the chemical could scrub out of the gas in some circumstances. The gas would then return to its odorless state.

Tim had come home and walked into a small sea of LP gas that had accumulated in his mobile home while he was at work. When he went to the refrigerator to look at some choices for dinner, the electric motor kicked on and the gas ignited.

That case took me quite a few years to complete. The terms of his settlement are confidential, but my fee was well into six figures on that case. Why did Tim come back to me? Because I treated him like a human being. I did a good job for him on his DWI. I let him know we were friends. I let him know I'd be there for him. Sure, he owed me a hundred dollars, and sure I could have used it, but as soon as you start chasing your client for fees after the case is over, you have lost him or her forever. When a case is over, you never know whether you will ever see that client again. If you treated them right, they can be a great source of referrals. If you have come to the end of their case and they still owe you money, they are most likely never going to pay you. They may come back though. If you chase them for the money, they will never come back or refer anyone to you. Give it some thought before you start chasing clients for fees you did not collect in time.

I hesitate to put this in print, but the truth is that if I get to the end of a case, and my clients have not paid all we agreed to, I tell them that I am forgiving the debt. First of all, the chances of them paying it are slim to none. Secondly, it makes them think I am a nice guy. They will remember that if they ever get in trouble again.

I once did a case for a very rich man who was in a lot of trouble. He was being sued by any number of people. He needed to file multiple suits against others. There were criminal charges filed, too. There was just a storm surrounding him. He was not only rich, he was famous. He had used many lawyers through his career.

When he came to me, I asked for and got a 25,000-dollar deposit that I put in my escrow account to secure my fees. He then paid my bill each month. I held the 25,000 dollars as insurance that my fees would be paid. When the cases drew to an end and we settled his final bill, he had a three thousand dollar balance in my escrow account. It goes without saying that I returned it to him as soon as the case was over.

I went on to represent him on other matters for almost twenty years, and he always made mention that I was the only lawyer he ever had who gave money back to him.

After practicing law for forty years, I have thousands of former clients. Those people send their friends and family members to me on a regular basis. Just today a young man came in with a new criminal case. He was referred by a lady he said was a friend of his father's. As it turned out, she is a woman who I represented almost fifteen years ago.

People like that are worth thousands of dollars in advertising dollars. Even though I know I'm not going to be practicing law forty years from now, I treat the new clients that I get today the same way I did when I first started practicing law. Those clients will continue to reward me with their loyalty.

Whether your clients are members of The Fortune 500 or the Unfortunate Five Million, you have to treat them all with the same level of respect. These people have chosen you above all other lawyers available. Stop and think about that for a minute. They had hundreds, maybe thousands, of lawyers to choose from. If you live in a small community where there are only five lawyers, they picked you over all the other lawyers. They are giving you the honor of entrusting you with their legal problem. They are standing next to you and saying, "This is my lawyer."

Their legal problem may only be a traffic ticket. You might have many open cases. I hope you do. But remember that they only have one. That traffic case is as important to them as any other case you have in your office. That is why you have to make up your mind that each of your clients is as important as the next. You cannot value your clients' worth simply by the amount of money they put in your bank account. I have terminated relationships with high paying clients when I did not feel I could give them the respect and representation they deserved. I treat all of my clients equally.

I respect my clients by being on time. I respect them by how I talk to them. I respect them by the way I treat them when they come into the office. Do not talk down to your clients just because they don't seem to understand. You can't expect them to understand the law. They hired you to explain the law to them, and sometimes that takes more time than you expect. Think about it this way: if it is taking a long time to explain, is it the listener or the talker who is not measuring up? Consider, though, that they have hired you to be their voice. They hired you to take care of their legal affairs. Take the time to explain how the law affects them as best you can. You are not going to make them understand all of it, and you can't expect them to, but you should make an effort.

I was once in a law firm with a guy who was a great lawyer, but he had no idea how to talk to lay people. He used a lot of jargon and legalese. It got to the point where he would have me come in with him when he talked to clients, so that I could serve as a kind of interpreter. No matter how hard he tried, he couldn't connect with the client. They would sit there and their eyes would glaze over while he spouted legal terms to them. He was technically a very good lawyer, but clients just did not relate to him. Not that he didn't respect the client; he just could not understand how to communicate with them. I am happy to say that he worked hard on changing his ways, and he is now a very successful attorney with many loyal clients.

On the other hand, I practiced law one time with a man who everybody loved. It didn't matter what the outcome of the case was, every client loved him. He was every client's friend. He respected those people. He respected them no matter what their background was, what their walk of life was. He treated them like royalty. You have to remember that these people are paying you money. They are the reason that you are practicing law, and they are human beings. They might be in a particular bad situation at that particular time, but they deserve to be respected. You should show them the same respect that you would like to have from others.

There are a couple of things you can do to make your client feel respected and taken care of. First of all, keep your clients informed. One of the complaints I hear all of the time is, "my lawyer doesn't return phone calls. I have no idea what's going on in my case." People constantly call me and want to change lawyers. They already have one, but they're not happy with him or her. I will talk with them, and I listen to their complaints about their attorneys. I tell them that they are not wrong in wanting more communication. Usually after I talk to them, I find absolutely no fault in what their lawyer is doing. Their lawyer just isn't keeping them informed. Then I tell them to call their lawyer and make an appointment. Go in and see the lawyer. I tell them to talk to their lawyer the way they have just talked to me. It generally works out.

Keep your clients informed. It is fairly simple. I send my clients copies of any pleadings that we file on their case. If I sent a letter to another lawyer or somebody else in their case, I send them a copy of that letter. I answer their phone calls when they call. In our phone system here, we don't screen our calls. Our calls come right to us. There is nothing to be gained by avoiding a client. He or she is your boss. Are they being a pain? Then ask yourself, "Why are you still representing them?" Ducking phone calls from clients gets you nowhere. You owe them your time. You agreed to that when you took on the case.

It is important. People want to know what's happening on their case. I even take the initiative and call them when they're not expecting a call from me. I'll call my clients in the evening because most of them are blue-collar people who are working every day. I can't reach them when they are out in the field, in the factory, at their job, so I'll call them in the evening just to give them an update. They deserve that. It is important and they're happy about that. This also keeps your clients from calling you at times that are inconvenient to you. This way, you take control of the situation. That actually works for your benefit. It helps to use your time wisely and it helps you serve your clients.

Another important thing is to be honest with your client. Don't create unreasonable expectations for them. There is nothing wrong with being encouraging. When the client comes in, tell them you are going to do your best. Tell them that you expect a good outcome on the case because you do. They do, however, deserve to know the truth. You have to be honest with them. Don't blow smoke at them. You have to give them a fair assessment of the case after you do a thorough investigation. They are looking to you for advice. I realize it is hard to give a negative assessment of a situation, but sometimes it is necessary.

I've taken in any number of medical malpractice cases that looked great when they started. The client will come in and tell a story. It can be about a terrible injury, or sometimes it is the death of a loved one. After we collect the medical records, have them reviewed by an expert, and spent a lot of time with them, we may find that there was no liability. It is hard to bring a client in and tell them that they have no case, but you owe them the truth.

It is difficult to tell a criminal client that he or she may be found guilty, but they have a right to know. It does not mean that you have not done your best to represent them. It is simply not a surety that you are going to win every case. Keep in mind that it is not your job to win at any cost. It is your job to give the best legal representation you can to the client. Sometimes that means you have to give them bad news. It is hard to do. They might not like it at the time, but in the long run, they're going to appreciate it.

My final advice on handling clients is to "fire yourself" if necessary. Just this morning, as a matter of fact, a lawyer stopped me in the hallway and told me he had taken some advice I had given him years ago. He had recently fired himself from a case. Every once in a while, you are going to find a client that you are not getting along with. That might be your fault and it may be their fault, but you know that the relationship is going nowhere. You are not getting the results they want, or maybe you are not getting the results you want. Your client's demands may be unreasonable. Your skills may be deficient. Whatever it is, you have to face up to the fact that you are in a situation that is not going to get any better. You are not going to be happy, and your client is not going to be happy.

Therefore, in a nice, polite and professional manner, terminate that relationship. Bring them into your office and explain to them that you don't feel up to handling the case. Don't blame them. Just tell them that you don't think that you are the right lawyer for them. Explain to them why not. Have their file ready for them, and return it to them. Have them sign a receipt for the file. Be careful, though, that you do not do something like this the week, or even the month, before the statute of limitations expires. You have to be mindful of that. Don't dump the case on them.

Here is another thing you should not do. Do not try to get out of a case right before trial just because you don't want to try the case. If you have taken the case up to the point that it is about to go to trial, try it or settle it. If you have not seen the necessity to get out of the case earlier, too bad for you. You do yourself and the profession a disservice by getting out of the case right before trial.

You will know when you have reached the point that you can no longer get along with the client. Your client is not happy with you, and you are not happy with working on the case. You are not doing yourself and your client any good by staying in that case. It might even mean you have to return some money. Do it. It will be worth it to you in the long run.

Sometimes, a client's demands are unreasonable. You might find that a client has misrepresented the facts to you. There might be times where you find that you are in over your head; the case isn't what you thought it was, you are not skilled enough to handle it, and you have let it sit there. The client starts calling and wants to know what is happening on their case (you will hear that question many times in your career), but you are putting the client off because you don't want to give them the bad news that it is more than you can handle. Get out of that case.

It may also happen that you develop a toxic relationship with a client. Very seldom is it anybody's fault. It is just one of those things that happens. One time, I took on a case with a lady who came in and said that she had been involved in an automobile collision where she was very seriously injured. She gave me an account of what happened, and I took her case.

We filed a lawsuit on it, but when we went to take the deposition for the case, she gave a totally different account of what happened. Not only did she give a different account, the way she described the accident in the deposition it could not even have physically happened. It became clear to me that she was making it up. She was trying to make the facts sound better than they were. She was telling the story the way she wanted it to have happened.

I brought her back to the office and I said, "Look, I can't in good conscious go forward with this lawsuit. You might find another lawyer who will go forward with it, but I can't. You are going to lose. Not only that, you are not even going to make it past the directed verdict." She wanted to continue on with the lawsuit, which was her right, but I couldn't do it, so I asked her to take her file back.

Firing yourself on a case is generally a product of not properly evaluating the case or the client in the first place. When people come in and talk to you about a case, they give you a fact situation, and with that fact situation, you have to evaluate the case. Then you have to determine what the legal issues are in that case. Sometimes, the clients have not intentionally misrepresented what took place, but they just have a view of things that is not quite accurate.

Once you have done an objective evaluation and investigation, and determined that that case is not what you thought it was when it came in, you have an obligation not to go forward on it. Your client may well pressure you to do so anyway. They may insist that they are right. The facts are what the facts are.

Your responsibility as a lawyer is to deal with the facts as they really are. If you determine that the facts are not what your client told you, it is your responsibility to discuss that with your client openly and honestly. Sometimes it is just a matter of perspective. I used to handle a high volume of automobile accident cases. It was not uncommon for parties in depositions in those cases to have totally different accounts of how the accident happened. The defense attorneys and I would sometimes talk during the break and discuss it. You would think that the people we were deposing were in completely different accidents.

If you find that the actual facts do not fit what the client has told you, then have a frank discussion about it. It may be that you cannot ethically go forward with the lawsuit. There is a distinction between a difference of opinion and an outright misrepresentation of the facts. Investigate and discover. Or, as Ronald Reagan used to say, "Trust but verify."

If you find that you cannot go on with a case, bring the client in, explain to them why you can't go forward with the lawsuit, and have the file prepared to give them. I make a copy of everything in their file. I give them their originals back, and then I terminate the relationship and explain to them that they should go see another attorney for an opinion if they want. You always want to be conscious of a thing like a statute of limitations when you are doing that, but there are just times that you have to fire yourself on a case. Have the client sign a letter or memo acknowledging that you are no longer their attorney. Keep that in your file. Make sure it is dated.

"Honesty is the best policy." It is hard to be the bearer of bad news. People do not want to hear that their case is not as good as they thought it was, but you will benefit in many ways if you are honest with your client. People who get that bad news might initially be unhappy with you. However, if you have been accurate about it, and they go to another reputable lawyer, they're going to find that you were right. They are not going to hold it against you. You owe this to yourself. You have to be determined early in your career to be honest and frank with your clients, and you should always avoid creating unreasonable expectations.

That does not mean that you avoid trying lawsuits unless they are slam-dunks. There is no way to predict the outcome of a lawsuit with certainty. Just because person has a legal right to recover, it does not necessarily guarantee that you are going to win the lawsuit. Do not think you are going to win every lawsuit. There is a very famous trial lawyer in America right now who used to brag about how he won all of his lawsuits in the past few years. He did get a lot of favorable jury verdicts in a row, but unfortunately, a number of them were taken away on appeal. So you decide; did he win or lose?

Let me make it clear. You owe a duty to these people. They have come to you. They have come to you for your legal knowledge and skill. The first question you must ask is whether they have a legal right to enforce or that has been violated? Then determine whether it is a case you want to pursue. It is not your job to win every lawsuit at any cost. It is your job to give legal advice to people. If you determine from the facts and the circumstances that they do not have a cause of action, tell them. If they do not have a defense, then you have to explain that to them. It is your obligation to do that. If you want to be a trial lawyer, then you must understand that you do not try cases just because people ask you to. You try cases because they are valid disputes that need resolution. You are going to feel a lot better about yourself.

Keep in mind that your clients are looking for an advocate. They are looking for an ally. They have come to you to be that person. That is true whether it is a real estate transaction, personal injury case, or family law matter. They are not only looking for an advocate, they're also looking for somebody who really cares about them. Remember that these people are in an area that is unfamiliar to them. They will benefit from your sincerity in dealing with them. They will be more comfortable because they feel you care about them. And that, my dear reader, will put money in your pocket. That is why you are reading this book, is it not?

Your clients are the ones who are going to make you successful. They are going to help you do what you want to do, which is practicing law and being successful at it. Treat your clients like you would your most valuable asset, because that is what they are. Give them the service that they deserve. Give them the respect that they deserve. Keep them informed, and they will pay dividends to you for the rest of your life.

Chapter 8
Legacy That Lasts

How to Win Clients, Their Kids and Their Kids' Kids!

Faithfulness comes in a lot of categories. This goes back to the last chapter on treating your clients as assets. When your client leaves your office and your case concludes, there is a great chance that you will never see that client again. For most people, ending up in a lawyer's office is an unusual situation. Some of my clients are repeat clients. However, the majority of my clients will only use a lawyer once in their lifetime. I do have a large number of repeat clients as well, but it is unusual for any one person to get seriously injured repeatedly. It is more common for certain people to be repeat offenders. I will see some people over and over again with criminal charges. But after a while they either grow out of that behavior or come to a tragic end. In my type of practice, I will generally have only one opportunity to serve any particular client.

So what do you want from your clients when they leave for the last time? First of all, you want them to remember you. You want them to remember you fondly. You want them to be loyal to you. You want them to refer their friends and family members to you when they are in need of legal services. Do not think that happens automatically.

Let me tell you something that happens way too often. It just blows my mind. I'll be in the middle of voir dire, and one of the questions that we generally ask is: "Have any of you ever been involved in a legal proceeding?" One or two will usually raise their hands. I ask, "Who was your lawyer?" I am amazed at the number of people who can't remember who their lawyer was.

One time, I asked a guy who was sitting in the jury panel if he had been involved in the legal system.

"Yes," was his answer.
"Do you mind telling me about it," I continued.
"I was charged with murder."
I said, "I assume you were found not guilty?"
"Oh yeah, I was," he said.
Who was your lawyer?" I asked.
"You know, I can't remember," he said.

It just astounds me. A person was represented by a lawyer in a murder trial and can't remember who that lawyer is. That lawyer really dropped the ball.

So how can you be faithful to your clients after they are gone? First of all, keep in contact with them. Remember these are just human beings like you are. Do you like it when you get a birthday card from someone? I do. Send them birthday cards. Send them Christmas cards. I am not going to get into the entire spectrum of religious holidays here. Christmas, Hanukkah, Ramadan, you get what I mean here. Let your former clients know that you still care about them. Pick up the phone sometime and give them a call. Remember, if we go back to the chapter on marketing, always be marketing. Just because a client isn't a client anymore, that does not mean that you can't keep in contact with them. These people are part of the fabric of your life. They are as much a part of your life as you are of theirs. You have shared a moment, a very specific experience, with these people. You have represented them in something that was important to them. It may be just a traffic ticket. It may be something more serious. It may have been routine. It may have been monumental. Whatever it was, it will always be part of your life's story, and you are part of theirs. Let them know that you still care about them because you do care about them. You were their friend. They were your friend.

Eventually, you may have thousands of people on your client list. If you apply what you learn in this book, you will. You are not going to be able to contact all of them all the time, but the little act of letting them know that you still remember them is important. I've got a couple of examples.

I had a really interesting thing happen just the other day. Recently an appellate court judge died. He was well known. There was a small article in the St. Louis Post-Dispatch about him when he died. It made mention of how he was a man of the people. He considered how his decisions would impact the people involved in the case.

He had been interviewed a few years prior to his death. In the interview, he mentioned a case of mine that he ruled on favorably. The Court overturned the conviction of an eighteen-year-old man who had been convicted of burglary. We got the case thrown because confession was illegally obtained. In the interview the judge said, "I still remember that case and I still wonder what happened to that boy." That case was in 1984, so it was that long ago, but that judge still remembered it.

It was about a week after I read the article about the judge's passing, that the boy (now a grown man) called me with a legal problem. I hadn't seen him since 1984, and out of the blue, just a strange coincidence, that man called me. Now, why did he call me? Because I had been his friend, and I had made him feel comfortable when I represented him. He called because I had kept in contact with him. For all those years, I sent him birthday cards and Christmas cards. I let him know I was there for him. That is why he came back to me with his legal problem.

Your clients, like all people, are going to go through good times and bad times. So what do you do when a client from the past calls you and is down on his or her financial luck? You represented them in the past. They paid your fee. Now they are going through a hard time and they need a lawyer. They have called you. But they cannot afford your usual and customary fee. In most cases, I give them a break. I work with them. I might put them on a payment program. I might even just give them a reduced fee. They are showing their loyalty to you. They still think you are a good lawyer. They have come back to you for help. The good things you do for them will come back to you tenfold.

You establish a unique relationship with every client you represent. You have a choice as to what that is going to be. That decision is yours. You create that relationship early on. If you view that client as a one-time client, he or she will be just that. You are in control. Will this person pass briefly through your professional life or will this person help you grow? If you are smart, you will make a decision that it is going to be a long-term relationship.

How do you do that? Spend some time talking to them about things other than their particular legal matter. Find out about their families. Do they have kids? Do they have siblings? What are their hopes and dreams for the future? These are not just clients. These are real people who want to be liked just like you do.

You might notice that one of your clients has a child who has won some award or sporting event. Send them a congratulatory note. Let them know you see them as more than just a source of money. It will pay off for you.

You will be surprised how often you get invited to weddings and, unfortunately, how often you get invited to funerals. That is, if your clients see you as a friend. Situations may occur where clients of old have children who need help. I recently got a call from a client who I represented over thirty years ago. His son had just got into a minor scrape, so he sent him to me.

You will bend over backwards to help those kids, just like you did for their parents. If you are lucky, you will be around to represent grandkids of your original clients. I have. When you do something special for a person's child, it is remembered. What you do for people's children is much more memorable than what you have done for them. It is a special blessing if you are building a practice, to be able to represent a former client's child. If your clients have that much faith in you, you can count yourself as a success.

All of these things that I'm telling you, pay off in the long run. You are not going to see the results next week, but I'm assuming that you are going to practice law longer than one or two years, and that you are in it for the long run. These things will pay off as long as you remember to do them.

Take the time to find out about your clients. Take the time to find out whether or not they have kids. Send them a note. Be vigilant. Read your local newspapers. Follow your clients on Facebook. Follow them, but remember that they see what you put on Facebook too, so be adult.

Facebook is a treasure trove of information about what your client's families are doing. When you see some announcement on there like, "My son just won the wrestling tournament," then take a minute and send them a little congratulatory card. (Remember the handwritten card?) The twelve-year-old boy isn't going to need a lawyer, but you can rest assured that that parent is going to remember you.

Once, I drove a hundred miles to go to a client's daughter's wedding. They were so appreciative that I was there that they took me around and introduced me to all their friends; "This was Donnie's lawyer. He's come all the way up here for his daughter's wedding." This was in a town that has a wonderful reputation for lawlessness. I was covered up with new business.

It is the same thing for funerals. I've driven hours to go to funerals of old clients, not because I'm trying to get business, but because I'm trying to show respect. Those people have honored me with their business. They have given me the opportunity to practice law for them and represent them. I honor them and their memories by going to their funerals. I don't feel obligated, but am always honored to do it. When people call me and tell me that one of my client's has passed away, or one of that one of my client's kids is having a wedding and I'm invited, that is an honor to me. We all practice law for money, but you can hold that money to your chest all you want and not feel the way you do when somebody honors you like that.

To sum up, here are some steps you can take to create a good, lifelong relationship with your client:

When your clients come to the office, let them know that you are concerned about them, their legal matter and their legal future. Do a good job for them. At the end of the case, let them know that you are there for them whenever they need you, and make them understand and believe that.

Afterwards, continue cultivating that relationship, if it is nothing more than sending birthday cards and Christmas cards.

When they call on you again for some type of legal service, be there for them. Be there for them in good times and in bad times. Let them know that you are there. Truly be their friend. Truly respect them and treat them like you'd want to be treated. Also: follow-up on that. Let them know how much you appreciate them, that you really are concerned about them, and then act that way.

The most important thing that I've done while building this legacy, aside from providing a good legal service and bonding with the clients, is keeping in contact with them. There are some clients that I have done more with. Some I've gone on hunting trips, fishing trips, and to ballgames, with.

There are clients that I have not represented for years that I'll call up and take to a baseball game. They are be so surprised and so happy to hear from me. I really am doing it just to catch up on their lives. We had a bond together. I am interested in what happens to them. I am interested in the stories of their lives.

I represent people all over the state of Missouri, so if I happen to be in their town on a court docket, I'll call them up and drop by and see them. I have clients that are in businesses in other towns, and without having represented them for years, I'll make a point of stopping by their business. For example, if they own a bar, I'll stop in and have a beer. If they own an insurance agency, I'll stop by and have some coffee with them. I really am happier when they own bars, but business is business.

It is simple human behavior. It is just about letting people know that you care about them. There is nothing tricky about it. It is the Golden Rule; treat people like you would like to be treated. They will appreciate it. Most of the people that you represent do not have a lawyer within their sphere of social contacts. They look at a lawyer as something special. They are proud to call a lawyer their friend. They are proud to have a friend as a lawyer, and my clients consider me to be their friends.

I'm not some guy who sits up on a pedestal in an ivory tower. I'm a guy that they can call on. People will call me at 8:00 or 9:00 at night just to ask a question. Does that bother me? Sure, sometimes. It is not necessarily even a case, but they'll have an issue that comes up that they'll want to know about. I give out my cell phone number to all of my clients. They can call me twenty-four hours a day because they are my best asset. They are my friends. I am their friend. They know that, so they trust me with their friends, their family, and heir kids. They know that I will do the best job possible for them and whoever they send to me. Whether it be a friend or a child or a grandchild, they are going to get good, caring, quality legal representation from somebody who really cares about them.

May it Please the Court

I know in my heart that you are better off for having read this book. All of the material in this book is tried and true. If you follow it, you will succeed. Success is more than just earning lots of money. Success is having a life that makes you glad to be alive everyday.

It isn't always easy, and there will be times when you will fall off the path. That is the way life is. That is the way people are. You will run into what we call blocks. With help you can overcome these blocks. These are the things that keep you from success. Financial security is a component of a happy life, but it is not everything.

That is one reason why I am a coach. I coach people who want to make their lives better and who are tired of talking about it, and want to take some action. People hire me as a coach to get results. Financial security is within your reach. It might be as simple as helping to develop a new practice area. It could be time management or changing the way you relate to your partners, co-workers, clients, or spouse. I coach people about everything from starting new businesses, to starting new ways to handle their caseload.

Here's the last piece of advice that I've got to offer: Learn what coaching is all about. It is not therapy for sick people; it is motivation for successful people who want to do more with their lives. Can I help you be a better person, lawyer, spouse, partner, or parent? Yes, I can. But you have to want it. You have to recognize you have been wishing you had it but haven't been able to get it. Give me a call. I will be glad to give you a free coaching session just because you bought this book. It may well be the best half hour you spend. If you just want to discuss things you have read here, I will do that too.

I believe my purpose is to have fun. I do that by helping people. It has given me a chance to live a life that is the envy of most people who know me. You ought to give it a try.

For more information, go to LiveBeyondFear.com or email me at: wayne@LiveBeyondFear.com

If you would be so kind, I would really appreciate it if you would go to amazon.com and write a review of this book. Your thoughts and feedback are important to me. Thank you.